A HISTORY OF MUSWELL HILL

by
Ken Gay

GW00481002

HORNSEY HISTORICAL SOCIETY

Published 1999

Reprinted with corrections 2000

by Hornsey Historical Society
The Old Schoolhouse
136 Tottenham Lane
London N8 7EL
ISBN 905794 25 7

Designed and typeset by Ministry of Design, Bath

Reset by Mike and Ruth Hazeldine

Contents

Acknowledgements

I am grateful to the Hornsey Historical Society for the use of its archive, where bound volumes of the *Hornsey Journal* from the 1880s are available, as well as other material. I am indebted to HHS member David Dell for the loan of a press cuttings book compiled by some past enthusiast which like my own similar volume (kindly given to me by Michael Maynard) contained many pertinent items, many from the *Muswell Hill Record*, including researched articles by F M W Draper on which I have drawn; it is a matter of regret that Dr Draper did not publish more than he did in book form.

In preparing the text I have drawn on research work I had undertaken for my chapter on The Limes estate in *People and Places – Lost Estates in Highgate, Hornsey and Wood Green*, the 1996 volume master-minded and edited by Joan Schwitzer for the Hornsey Historical Society. But I have tried not to repeat too much of that information. I have also tried to avoid covering topics dealt with, often in great detail, by Jack Whitehead in his 1995 volume *The Growth of Muswell Hill*, especially his account of Collins's activities.

Like many Middlesex historians I am indebted to the *Victoria County History of Middlesex*, in particular volume VI which includes Hornsey. This greatly reduces the need for much research work in providing both facts and sources. Otherwise I list below the maps, documents and books I have consulted. I decided to abandon the academic practice of footnotes giving sources as I think the reader can fairly easily ascertain from the Source list where I obtained my information. I might also add that a close physical knowledge of Muswell Hill, its nooks and crannies, architecture and landscape is a must for anyone trying to write a detailed local history and over the years I have tried to explore every road in Muswell Hill.

I would like to thank Joan Schwitzer, president of the Hornsey Historical Society once again for the invaluable guidance she gives me in local history, a professional association which now goes back over twenty years of society membership. Peter Barber, chairman of the society, has provided local knowledge and his cartographical expertise in his capacity of Deputy Map Librarian at the British Library. Malcolm Stokes made valuable comments on the text, especially on the mediaeval period. Other members of the society's Publications Committee have also helped and I would like to thank Albert Pinching, Elizabeth Israel and Ruth and Michael Hazeldine.

List of Illustrations

I acknowledge with thanks the loan of illustrations from the collections of Hornsey Historical Society (HHS), the London Borough of Haringey at Bruce Castle (BC), the London Metropolitan Archive (LMA), Anthony Edmondson and John Farr (AE/JF), Arthur Reynolds (AR), Hugh Garnsworthy (HG), and Dick Whetstone (DW). Those uncredited in the list below are from my own collection. As far as possible I have avoided using the illustrations which I included in the two picture books *Highgate and Muswell Hill – Chalford Archive Photographs Series* by Joan Schwitzer and Ken Gay and *From Highgate to Hornsey: A portrait in old postcards* by Ken Gay and Dick Whetstone.

Preface

This is about the place in which I have lived for forty five years, and I sometimes ponder on the chance that brought me to the area. I think the story begins for me in November 1948 when, having seen a small advertisement, I went one night to an international friendship club in Kensington Square, one of those get-together places surviving from the recent war. At that Saturday night dance I met Teresa. Five years later, all too long after, she agreed to marry me.

Those were the days of 'proper behaviour' and we sought somewhere to live before we arranged the wedding. Teresa was living with a girl friend in a furnished flat in Belsize Park and I had returned recently to my family home in Forest Gate, east London, after some years of absence. I registered with a South Kensington accommodation agency and had their daily list of vacant flats sent to me at the office where I worked. As soon as I got the lists I phoned up anything suitable. The flats were all over London and we might just as easily have settled in Kingsbury, Acton or Kilburn as come to Muswell Hill area, but we didn't.

After visiting several flats the search ended when Teresa and I met at the end of an afternoon outside a promising address. We had managed to be the first ones there and when we told the landlady that we wanted to get married she let us have it. There was no question of her looking for a better paying tenant, for in those days the weekly rent was 'controlled'. Teresa moved in right away, after we had gathered together some furniture from friends and family, and three weeks later, in February 1954, our wedding took place and we set up home there.

It was in this way that we came to live in the Borough of Hornsey, for the flat was at 211 Archway Road, not far from Highgate tube station, just past the turning called Cholmeley Park. It was one of about ten Victorian houses of circa 1870 set back behind a front garden and screened from the road by trees. In 1954 some of these houses were somewhat neglected (no painting of houses took place during the war and for some years afterwards due to shortage of materials). Our flat was on the top floor and I often wonder if it was my heavy-handed way with a vacuum cleaner that led to the ceiling of the flat below falling down. We watched it from our window being carried out into the front garden on the carpet. Nothing was ever said. In the basement flat lived Caribbean novelist John Hearne, whose first half-dozen books were mostly written in the 1950s. Although it was nine years after the war, rationing was still in place for some foods and Teresa and I registered for our meat ration at the butcher's just up the hill. But it was a wonderful time that spring of 1954. It was then that Teresa and I got to know the pleasures of Highgate village, culminating in visits to Kenwood and its superb collection of paintings, where we often took visiting friends.

By summer Teresa was pregnant with our first child. We knew we wanted a house, not easy to get on a modest income and with a post-war housing shortage. Teresa was a teacher in Islington, myself in a nationalised industry headquarters in Victoria, so our choice was limited. One day we crossed busy Archway Road from our flat to the parade of shops opposite and went to the offices of estate agent Edmund Cude, on the corner. Elderly Mr Cude was kind, but did not offer us what we wanted. We ended up with Mr Alfred Slinn, whose estate office, known as the White House and today still used as an estate agency, juts out onto the pavement at the top of Muswell Hill. There an energetic young Mr Dennell (who subsequently set up his own Crouch End firm) negotiated a price for a 1929 house in Alexandra Park; three bedrooms, one cellar and a long garden. The price was £2,700 (yes, £2,700 not £270,000). On 23rd August 1954 we moved in, just too late to use Alexandra Palace branch railway which sadly closed in July between our seeing the house and our buying it.

Here I still live, though Teresa died in February 1997, after 43 years of marriage. The house was then in the Borough of Wood Green (it became Haringey in 1965) but we found that Muswell Hill was our gravitational local centre for shopping and soon we were pushing a pram through what is now called the Broadway (from 1960). Teresa was later to teach in Muswell Hill at Tetherdown primary school in Grand Avenue.

In the late 1970s Liz Luxmore, Muswell Hill librarian, was a prime mover in arranging Festivals for Muswell Hill, with stalls in the sloping car park and processions and events. In 1977, at one of these stalls, Teresa and I became members of the Hornsey Historical Society, a decision which led us to make many friends. Curiosity took hold, and gradually I wanted to find out more about Muswell Hill. With retirement I found more scope for this and the text which follows results mainly from my curiosity about the place where I had come to live. I hope it may be of interest to other residents.

Chapter 1

Beginnings

It's the geography that affects you, rather than its history, when you first come to Muswell Hill. In our honeymoon days in Highgate we walked down Shepherds Hill to Crouch End Broadway and loved its nestling quality, in the hollow of cross roads and with interesting shops. But when we went up to Muswell Hill, walking our way between the two woods, we loved the heights and windyness and the views. One of my favourite looking-places is still at the top of Hillfield Park on the Broadway, looking down over the Thames Valley and seeing the vast panoply of London spread out, at its core that bunch of tall office blocks crowding round the dome of St Paul's Cathedral. Or from outside the Green Man looking towards the Lea valley, or walking from Colney Hatch Lane down Alexandra Park Road and turning its corner by St Andrew's church seeing the Lea valley again, with far away tower blocks thrusting up against the ridge of Epping Forest. Muswell Hill is height and it kept itself to itself till the end of the nineteenth century, a rural retreat enjoyed most by those who lived in that dozen or so detached villas, set in their own grounds, that once dominated the landscape.

Geography is an important determinant of history, I was taught at school, and in the history of Muswell Hill we can see all the factors at work. It stands at the edge of a plateau (formed by glacial deposits from the last Ice Age) and its hilly nature, with streams running off to the valley to the east, helped deter major roads from crossing it. (Not so in Tottenham where the Romans laid down a military route to Lincoln along the Lea valley which later helped the growth of an urban village along its line). So difficulty of access determined settlement. So too did the soil, a heavy clay which meant that arable farming with larger populations needed for it, was not developed in place of less labour-intensive pasture farming i.e. grazing animals and producing hay. Before the farming the trees had to be cleared, for the same clay soil had favoured the spread in prehistoric times of what came to be called the Great Middlesex Forest, over the land north of the river Thames.

The Thames was of course the other major factor determining what happened here, some six miles north. The Thames provided a deep natural harbour, one of the main keys to the history of the British Isles, set at a nodal point in the globe. Trade was to be from here to the Baltic, the Rhine, the Mediterranean and then across the Atlantic and eastern seas and oceans around the world. Thus was established the wealth and power of London and the area around it became its hinterland, providing food, labour, feed for its horses and for the better off a place to escape to, to invest in, to own property. Muswell Hill has always been under the influence of London, serving London's needs, and its history can only be understood in relation to this.

Where can we set that history to begin? The known history of our area begins with the earliest written medieval records and it would be safest to start there. But one has to ask what happened before the written records and to consider what archeological finds might suggest to us. Originally people of the Neolithic, Bronze and Iron ages might have been in the area. As a testimony to Bronze Age people's presence is a flint dagger found in Hornsey in the 19th century, the exact site of its discovery not recorded. For early peoples the wooded Northern Heights (as our location has been known) could have provided defensible shelter and perhaps the first ridge paths and tracks could have been made.

The Romans arrived in Britain with the Claudian invasion of AD43 to make the island an imperial province. By AD55 the Thames had been bridged at the place where then the tide turned and Londinium established on its two gravel hills amongst the shallows and marshes of the river. The famous Roman roads were made by first cutting wide swathes through the forests to minimise the danger of attack whilst they were being built. Ermine Street (now the line of Tottenham High Road) to the east and Watling Street (now the line of Edgware Road) to the west were the main routes north. What other roads, connecting the two were made, if any? None have been positively identified and indeed there is no evidence of Roman settlement in the area probably because the poor soil would have helped deter this, but there are some discovered artefacts indicating some Roman presence.

In Highgate Wood, between Muswell Hill and Highgate, the remains of a seasonal Roman pottery have been excavated; by what route was its product brought for sale in London? Nearby, where Highgate Library was built in Shepherds Hill, a bronze sword handle and pot containing coins (now lost) were found c.1830-50. Two vessels, possibly 1st century and tile fragments were found in 1970 in Southwood Lawn Road. In Cranley Gardens not far away was found in 1928 a buried Roman pot. It contained 654 coins from circa AD 209, a bronze ring and a silver spoon, now in the British Museum. Was it buried in the forest by a worried Roman or was it military money? Other scattered Roman coins, such as the fourth century coin of Constantine the Great, found in 1927 in Barrenger Road, Muswell Hill, remind us of the Roman period.

The Roman forces left in the fifth century AD to try unsuccessfully to stave off the collapse of their western empire. A strong migration of people from northern Europe to these islands developed, part of many migrations of peoples taking place across Asia and Europe. Known as the Anglo-Saxons they were famously described by Bede in 731 in his *Historia Ecclesiastic Gentis Anglorum* in the Roman language of Latin.

Archeological work continues to establish more factual knowledge about this period. A museum of London 1998 publication (*London Bodies*) refers to the 'origin myths' from historians like Bede and says that these 'plus past and present day ethnic-labelling make it difficult to sift through and separate the strands of accurate record from constructed history'; 'archeology suggests cultural change, with people adopting and adapting different ways of living.' The incomers would of course have found a settled Romano British people with their own culture patterns.

It would seem, however, that these immigrants, using a language which came to be called Old English, began to settle, farm, give place names, develop a road system and establish boundaries of land ownership, manors and later, parishes. Names, boundaries and roads are legacies from the past which last much longer than buildings or even human reputations. The basic shaping of our local history of settlement emerges from these long ago centuries, affecting us today.

Place names in Middlesex, Hertfordshire and Essex mostly date from pre-Norman Conquest times, and are subject to interpretation; spelling was not standardised and pronunciation can vary. Local historian Dr S J Madge considered that the place name of the manor, and later parish, in which Muswell Hill was situated derived from the old English words *Heringes-hege* (with g pronounced as a y) said to mean the enclosure of Haering or of Hering's people. From this root the names of Haringey and Hornsey came and in 1936 Dr Madge published an account of about 160 variants of the name found in documents. Harringeie by Tudor times was being corrupted into Harnsey and Hornsey and it was the latter spelling which was to become established by the eighteenth century as the parish in which Muswell Hill was.

Saxon immigration would have been by boat across the North Sea and then possibly by river valley or river to penetrate forests and to create farmsteads and settlements. The inference of the name is that a clearing was established, perhaps for pasture or to prevent domesticated animals from straying. Possibly this original settlement was near where Hornsey church was later built with the settlement's name being given to the manor. No manor house seems to have existed locally.

If you stand on the south terrace of Alexandra Palace you can see the surviving medieval tower of Hornsey church and the valley where this settlement is thought to have started. Just north of the tower was a small river, draining into the Lea further east, providing an essential water supply, later known as the Moselle. The immigrants, who became the dominant people in the south of Britain were essentially farmers looking for land, rather like some immigrants to North America in later centuries, or those invading South Africa, Australia, New Zealand and elsewhere. The Saxons established subsistence farming, and intermarried with the local British over time. The results are to be seen through the pages of Domesday Book a few centuries later, which in 1086 summarised the economy of the country. Livestock, including herds of swine feeding on forest acorns would be an important element. Clearance of forest was limited, for about half the parish was still wooded in the Tudor era.

Muswell Hill was to have two place names. One was Pinnsknoll, in various spellings, which was seen by Dr Madge as being a difficult name to interpret but that its probable meaning was 'Pinn's knoll or summit, from the personal name of Pinn'. Other interpretations have been made, such as a derivation from a Saxon word for chaffinch. It must be emphasised that it was the hill which was named not a road a settlement. This is true of the other name, Muswell Hill. Madge says that during the fifteenth and sixteenth centuries the name of Muswell Hill became fixed, though the name Pinnsknoll appeared in manorial rolls for some time afterwards. Muswell Hill as a name derives not only from the hill but from its springs or wells, from which issued the Muswell Stream which ran down the hill and along the line of present day Albert Road (not to be confused with the Moselle mentioned above). The wells were located about where present day No. 40 Muswell Road is now built. The first element of the name Muswell emerged from the Old English word *meos* meaning moss and the second from the Old English word *wielle* meaning well, fountain or spring, according to Madge, so rendering the name to mean 'the hill of the mossy spring'. The name probably became prominent when the well water was seen as holy from the twelfth century, as explained later. Variant spellings recorded are Mussell Hill (1631), Muzzle Hill (1641) and Muscle Hill (1746).

Boundaries of estate ownership and systems of local government, as well as place names seem to date from before the Norman invasion of 1066. The manorial system, later taken over and developed by the Normans, is of Saxon origin. This hierarchical system is based on the pre-eminence of the lord of the manor who held the land, with various types of tenure, rights and obligations controlled by him; customs were enforced and tenure endorsed by a Court Baron, and conduct and jurisdiction by a Court Leet. Muswell Hill was an area within the Manor of Hornsey whose lord was the Bishop of London. It is not listed separately in Domesday Book (as Tottenham manor is) as it was part of the Bishop's larger manor of Stepney, although by 1241 it was accounted for separately by a reeve (a deputy officer who ran the business of the manor). The date when the manor of Hornsey was established and its boundaries laid down is unknown but it was owned by the Bishop of London before the Norman Conquest. This ownership of land continued down the centuries, passing to the Ecclesiastical Commissioners in 1868, subsequently the Church Commissioners. The church in consequence has been an important local landowner down to modern times, though much has been sold off.

The creation of a Bishopric followed of course the conversion of the southern pagan tribes in England to Christianity. The Celtic west, particularly Ireland was Christian by the early sixth century but in the south of England conversion began with the arrival in AD 597 on the Kent coast of (St) Augustine and his 40-strong mission. Sent by the Pope his success depended upon the conversion of local kings in a divided island of separate kingdoms with small populations. This was successful over a period of time and a system of church government evolved, with monasteries or 'ministers' which by the eighth century were becoming numerous and developing pastoral work among local communities, providing baptism and burial rites and receiving from them tithes, a tax for the church allowed by the king.

Defined parishes emerged in this way, for which existing manorial boundaries were taken into account. Parish boundaries and manorial boundaries could coincide and this seems to have been the case with Hornsey. Parishes seem to have led to the first English local churches and Hornsey parish church is to be found in the north east corner, probably because this was the original settlement and there may even have been a pagan precursor. When Hornsey parish was established, and when its first church was built is not known. The first record of St Mary's, the parish church of Hornsey dates from 1291, when with other English churches, it was assessed for ecclesiastical taxation. The first record of a priest and a rectory is 1302, with the living in the gift of the Bishop of London from at least 1321. (The parish in truncated form still exists to this day, known as St Mary-with-St George since, following the demolition of the last parish church on the old site, it amalgamated with St George's in Cranley Gardens.)

Regarding Hornsey manor, some time before the Conquest the Stepney manorial lands were divided between the Bishop of London and the Cathedral Chapter at St Paul's, with Hornsey manor remaining with the bishop and Brownswood manor in the south under the control of the Prebendary of St Paul's. Subsequent bishops created sub-manors out of Hornsey manor, such as Fernfields manor between Hornsey village and Crouch End which eventually came under the bishop of Exeter, and Topsfield manor at Crouch End. As far as Muswell Hill is concerned an important allocation of land was made by the bishop of London in 1152, as I shall describe.

In later centuries control of local affairs was to pass from the manorial courts to the parish vestries. These in the nineteenth century were to be replaced by new forms of local government better equipped to deal with the needs of much larger populations. Nevertheless it is interesting to note that the present day London Borough of Haringey has boundaries very similar to the combined ancient manors of Hornsey and Tottenham, evolved a millennium ago, so the amount of council tax we pay is determined by boundaries evolved in late Saxon times, such is the long reach of history. (The boundaries are not altogether the same; detached portions in the south, for example were absorbed into Stoke Newington, now the London Borough of Hackney, as was South Hornsey, south east of Finsbury Park). But boundaries tend to persist.

Roads, as well as place names and boundaries, are the other medieval legacy affecting the layout of Muswell Hill and other local places. Human pathways are one of the constant survivors of the past. Small settlements developed within Hornsey not only by the church but south at Crouch End and to a limited extent at Stroud Green, and to the west at Muswell Hill and Highgate. These were all linked by early roads which survive today. Names for roads did not become fixed until the development in the 19th century of the postal system and the same road could have different names. These road names were frequently associated with their destination.

London was an important nodal point for roads and one that ran to and from the north followed the line of the Stroud Green Road and Crouch Hill, through Crouch End, along what was once Maynard Street but which is now called Park Road, then up the hill and along Colney Hatch Lane to Whetstone and onwards. In the 1816 Hornsey Enclosure Award the road is called Hornsey Road as it went up the hill till it went along 'the old gravel road', that is Colney Hatch Lane to the parish boundary to the north of Muswell Hill.

1. This view down Muswell Hill was drawn in 1822 by T.M.Baynes (1794 – 1852) from a point near The Green Man.

2. The Green Man photographed in 1879. A brick hotel extension was to replace the building on the right.

Unfortunately this road was often deep in mud in winter and rutted in summer and generally in poor condition, due in part to the streams which drained down onto it from the Highgate ridge. John Norden in his Middlesex section of his *Speculum Britanniae*, published in 1593, said that this road was so bad that another route developed out of Holloway up Highgate Hill, to carry on northwards through Barnet. This was only after the Bishop of London had given permission for the road to cross his large hunting park (which stretched as far north as present day Grand Avenue.)

The bishop was charging a toll by 1319 and Highgate grew as a settlement. The name Highgate is however earlier than the toll and derives from Heygate or Heghgate (haia meaning a hedge and gata meaning a road), meaning the road through the hedge surrounding the bishop's park. Later interpretations of the name have taken it to mean, erroneously, High toll gate. Highgate developed on the boundary between Hornsey and St Pancras, which ran down the section known as the High Street; today this is the boundary between Haringey and Camden. This road through Highgate became a main route for drovers and other travellers and the settlement overshadowed that at Muswell Hill with its inadequate road to the north. A survey of licensed victuallers in 1552 showed that Highgate had five compared with only one for Muswell Hill (and three for Hornsey). Refreshment was a natural roadside provision and many isolated public houses across England demonstrate. The Muswell Hill alehouse would most likely have been The Green Man, conveniently situated at the top of what was once a much steeper hill and at the turning point for the road going north.

This turning point was also the junction with another ancient route which ran from Muswell Hill south to Highgate (and probably originally to Kilburn Priory). It was appropriately named Southwood Lane, which the section west of Archway Road is still called. The section from Muswell Hill was called Muswell Hill Road from the mid-nineteenth century, whereas the 1816 Enclosure Award refers to it as Southwood Lane or Hornsey Lane Road. Till the end of the nineteenth century there were no other roads joining this junction; Queens Avenue and Dukes Avenue are additions dating from 1897 and 1900 respectively. The name Muswell Hill Road was retained by the shopping centre until 1960 when it was renamed Muswell Hill Broadway; today Muswell Hill Road refers to the section south from St James's church only.

The south side of this ancient road, where Marks and Spencer and other shops stood in the 1990s was open land known as Muswell Hill Common. This area between Muswell Hill, Muswell Hill Road (now Broadway) and St James's Lane attracted unauthorised settlers as common land often does, and cottages were built on the edge of the common in St James's Lane. This became a small village settlement, nestling down in the hollow, known by some locals I have met as 'the old village'. The common transferred into private ownership under the 1816 Hornsey Enclosure Award, with some properties later built alongside the Muswell Hill Road, but it remained largely open until towards the end of the nineteenth century.

Another ancient route led to East Finchley, a settlement which grew up when the new road to the north, having gone through the bishop's park, exited there. In the 1816 Hornsey Enclosure Award it is referred to as Fortis Green Road or Finchley Common Road, the common being not far to the north of East Finchley. The origin of the name Fortis Green is obscure, according to the English Place Name Society. It is recorded in Hornsey manorial court rolls in 1613 as Fortessegreene. In his 1754 map of Middlesex John Rocque labels it Forty Green but the 1816 Award calls it Fortis Green (Fortis House was the name of an important Muswell Hill property).

From the junction of Fortis Green and Fortis Green Road (the route is now two separately named roads) another road, also ancient in origin, leads north. For many years this led to Coppetts Farm and to the valley of the Bounds Green brook (today the route of the North Circular Road). The 1816 Award calls this Hornsey Common Road 'beginning at Fortis Green, leading along the new gravel road over the east side of Hornsey Common to the lower end thereof near Irish corner'. Hornsey Common lay on the west side of this route, incorporating the huge Coldfall Wood and stretching towards Finchley Common, notorious in the eighteenth century for highwaymen.

Towards the end of the nineteenth century this road was known as Tatterdown Lane and began to be lined on this west side by later Victorian houses. Councillors were not happy with the name and invented in about 1893 Tetherdown as a new name for it, though the group of mid-Victorian cottages which stand where Tetherdown merges with Coppetts Road on the corner of Pages Lane were known as Tatterdown Place; sometime later they came to be known as Victoria Cottages.

Coppetts Farm building dated from 1670 and survived until 1933. Its site is now occupied by a block of flats built between Wilton and Sutton Roads laid out over the farmland. Pages Lane seems to have originated as a narrow back lane connecting the Hornsey Common road with ancient Colney Hatch Lane. It was variously named Red House Lane, Jones Lane and now Pages Lane. In earlier centuries it was narrower than it is today.

These Muswell Hill roads were all established by the sixteenth century at the latest, and define the area. Their routes are older than any surviving buildings in Muswell Hill. They were the spinal framework to which the residential roads were added in the late nineteenth and early twentieth centuries when Muswell Hill was built up as a suburb. Among these new residential roads is the comparatively long Creighton Avenue driven through ancient Coldfall Wood in 1900 as a feed road to the new development.

Today as we stand at Muswell Hill roundabout by the swirl of traffic nothing seems ancient, or at least not much more than a century or so old. But the line the traffic follows is very old, perpetuating routes that once wended their way through ancient forest, portions of which still remain in the form of Highgate Wood and adjacent Queens Wood. Stand by the Green Man and remember it was once an old alehouse for medieval travellers in centuries many of us cannot visualise at all.

Chapter 2

The Medieval use of Muswell Hill Lands

The first written record of Muswell Hill as a place dates from the twelfth century when the bishop of London, as lord of the manor of Hornsey granted some land. The twelfth century was a great age for institutional Christianity in Europe and the foundation and expansion of many religious orders. Newly established on the outskirts of London in Clerkenwell was the priory of St Mary, a house of Augustinian canonesses founded circa 1145 by Jordan de Bricet who also established near it the house of the Knights Hospitallers of St John of Jerusalem. Within fifty years of its foundation the priory had widespread possessions in the south of England. Among the earliest lands they acquired was through a grant made by Richard de Belmeis, bishop of London from 1152 until his death in 1161. The original charter, probably made in 1152, is mentioned in a surviving confirmatory charter of Archbishop Theobald, apparently made soon afterwards:

> 'know all ye that we have hearkened to the just applications of Christiana the prioress and other holy ones of the church of the Blessed Mary of Clerkenwell.......according to the tenor of the charter of our venerable brother Richard, bishop of London they now possess....to wit these possessions of the land of Mosewelle and the land which Jordanus lord of that foundation gave and granted them.....'

This is the first known written record of Muswell Hill.

The land granted, a detached portion of Clerkenwell parish, lay on the east side of present day Colney Hatch Lane and was probably undeveloped roadside manorial land. It occupied some 64 acres, the site being in terms of present day roads, between about Dukes Avenue in the south and Goodwyns Vale in the north. Eastward it stretched to the former Hornsey manor boundary with the manor of Tottenham.

This eastern boundary can still be identified on the spot today by the metal markers at ground level which can be found in Dukes Avenue, Muswell Road, Donovan Avenue and other roads. These markers were erected in 1934 by the Borough of Hornsey to mark the boundary with Wood Green which had been created a borough in 1933 (Wood Green being formerly a part of Tottenham).

The Augustinian Canonesses of St Mary Clerkenwell were also granted land in Tottenham between 1165 and 1176 and this might well have been adjacent to the Muswell Hill property for it consisted of some 140 acres in the 'hanger' of Tottenham. This would have been Tottenham Wood which till the eighteenth century covered the hilly land now occupied by Alexandra Park. This was to be one of Tottenham's largest monastic estates and it and the Clerkenwell Detached land were both to be retained until the 1539 Dissolution of religious houses.

The Muswell Hill land was developed by the nuns as a farm and is an early example of London's hinterland being used for food production by those living in the inner area. The story is given by John Norden in *Speculum Britanniae* (the 38 page quarto treatise of 1539):

> '*At Muswell Hill, called also Pinsenell Hill, there was a Chapel here sometime bearing the name of Our Ladie of Muswell, where now Alderman Roe hath erected a proper house, for there is on the hill a spring of faire water, which is nowe within the compasse of the house. There was sometime an image of the ladie of Muswell, whereunto was a continuall resort, in the way of pilgrimage, growing as (though I take it) fabulously reported, in respect of a great cure which was performed by this water, upon a king of Scots, who being strangely diseased, was by some divine intelligence advised to take the water of a well in England called Muswell, which after a long scrutation, and inquisition, this well was found and performed the cure; absolutely to denie the cure I dare not, for that the high God hath given virtue unto waters, to heal infirmities, as may appeare by the cure of Naaman the leper.*'

Although Norden does not seem to know the king's name he was identified by Dr F M W Draper in his pamphlet *Muswell Farm or Clerkenwell Detached* (1934) as being Malcolm IV who ruled from 1153 to 1165 and died at the age of 24. Neighbouring Tottenham manor was for some time in the possession of the Scottish royal house (the name of Bruce Castle for the Tottenham manor house is a reference to this period) and Malcolm had granted the Tottenham hanger lands to Robert of Northampton on condition that he left them to the nuns of Clerkenwell Priory. (Relevant charters are included in the priory cartulary i.e. its register of lands and privileges). So Norden's 'long scrutation and inquisition' might be a dramatic heightening of the story.

The fame of the cure spread and Muswell Hill in the middle ages drew pilgrims to take the water of the springs, perhaps in the same way as in modern times at Lourdes in France where pilgrims seek cures, although in those days of very small populations and poor transport not on anything like the same scale of today. Pilgrimages seem to have usually been made in August and in time 'indulgences' were sold, a system which grew up during the Crusades whereby sinners were granted remission of temporal penalties. Undoubtedly the system was abused and was one of the features attacked by church reformers. Pilgrimages themselves were not always made in a pious spirit, as William Pinks maintains in his *History of Clerkenwell*. Offerings by pilgrims were a source of income for the priory, calculated in 1535 as about two pounds per annum, a large sum in those days, although the total annual income of the Priory of Clerkenwell was over £227 in that year.

The nuns' ownership of the farm and all their other lands, came to an end in 1539 when Henry VIII declared himself head of the English church and seized church lands. The prioress was required to demise the estate to the king's bottler, John Avery. It then included a farmhouse, gatehouse, house, storehouse and a chapel. No map is known depicting the layout of the farm and it might well be that it extended across Colney Hatch Lane to include land on the west side (though Clerkenwell Detached was wholly on the east side). It was on the west side of the lane, where a Roman Catholic Church was built in the 1930s, that a headless statue was excavated whilst the church was being built and identified as a statue of St Mary dating from the 13th century. So the chapel might have been here, conveniently near the lane, rather than a few hundred yards away adjacent to the well. But this of course is speculation as, unfortunately, no archeological excavations have taken place in this area, despite the fact that little except a few detached villas were built here.

After its acquisition in 1539 the nuns' land remained as Clerkenwell Detached, under the jurisdiction of St James's church in Clerkenwell, which stood adjacent to the priory. Clerkenwell Detached is so marked on the first Ordnance Survey maps of the nineteenth century, with an acreage of 64.452. Jurisdiction was asserted by Clerkenwell parish on the grounds that the nuns had not paid tithes (ecclesiastical taxes) to the Rector of Hornsey. Under the tithe system a tenth part of the main crops from the land such as corn, wood etc, was paid to the local vicar. (The system was altered to a rental charge by the Tithe Commutation Act of 1836 and finally abolished a century later.) The existence of this separate authority for a portion of Muswell Hill did not seem to cause problems until urbanisation in the late nineteenth century when disputes over sewage disposal and other local authority concerns caused friction. Once again the long reach of history from the twelfth to the nineteenth century brought unforeseen results. Some claimed that Muswell Hill's urban development was held back by the anomaly of two authorities for the area.

The wells which gave Muswell Hill its name existed until the end of the nineteenth century. Pinks in the 1880 edition of his Clerkenwell *History* described them as:

'two in number, and continue in good preservation, being bricked round to the depth from which they seemingly spring (about five feet and a half) and enclosed from the field where they are situated by wooden railings. Though only a few yards asunder, their water differs in quality; that of one being hard, sweet and beautifully pellucid, while the other more nearly resembles rain water and is used only for the purposes for which the latter is applied. Neither is supposed to possess any medicinal properties. By the united and ceaseless overflowing of these wells, a rivulet is formed and named after them the Mose or Moselle, which descending the hill takes a devious course through the parishes of Hornsey and Tottenham.....eventually it finds its way into the River Lea at Broadmead Marsh.'

When the fields began to disappear towards the end of the nineteenth century Clerkenwell considered preserving the wells. But this idea seems to have been lost when in 1900 Clerkenwell Detached became part of Hornsey under legislation allowing the adjustment of boundaries. Other wells fed from the same underground springs existed in Muswell Hill, used by the larger houses for water supply in the days before an urban piped water supply. Interestingly a well was discovered in 1999 when building work was taking place at No. 3 Colney Hatch Lane, the early nineteenth century villa which stands next to the Roman Catholic Church (built on the site of No. 1).

Ownership of the farm passed into private hands, the priory at Clerkenwell being dissolved. On 6th September 1539 Richard Layton wrote to Thomas Cromwell: 'we put the Duke of Norfolk's servant in custody of Clerkenwell and have fully dissolved it to the contention of the prioress and her sisters'. Thomas Cromwell, Earl of Essex (1485-1540) had been made vicar general under the Act of Supremacy of 1534 and sought to abolish papal supremacy, and reform the church, beginning with Acts of 1536 and 1539 for the dissolution of the monasteries, showing the monarch how to dispose of the ecclesiastical lands at a cheap rate to the laity, thereby winning self-interested support for the king's policy of social change. Cromwell, who held many high offices, was unscrupulous in using his official positions to acquire property for himself. Incurring wide enmity he lost the king's support and was beheaded on Tower Hill in July 1540. The properties of the priory were separately granted away. The last prioress Isabell Sackville received an annual pension of £50 which she enjoyed for over 30 years, dying in July 1570. The other nuns received pensions.

The Muswell Hill change of land ownership was only a tiny part of a national great change. Francis Sheppard has pointed out in his *London – A History* (Oxford University Press 1998) that between 1536 and 1542 all of London's thirty or so religious houses were dissolved, including the Knight's Hospitallers in Clerkenwell and half a dozen houses of Augustinian canons and canonesses. Through the dissolution of the monasteries, Sheppard says, the Crown obtained a substantial amount of land around the city of London which allowed new suburbs to be built in due course, although some of the land survives today in the shape of St James's Park, Green Park, Hyde Park and Regent's Park. Crown Estate Commissioners still administer the area of Piccadilly, Jermyn Street, Pall Mall and Carlton House Terrace, though much of the Crown's sixteenth century acquisitions were dispersed, being acquired by aristocrats such as the Russells and the Earl of Southampton.

The outward expansion of the original city in land terms was to be matched by its population growth, rising, Sheppard records, from about 75,000 in 1550 to 200,00 in 1600. By 1650 it had risen to 400,00 and by 1700 to about 575,000. This sevenfold increase in 150 years was not matched in the rest of England, Sheppard says, where the population did not even double. The rise of London's population has not been adequately explained, argues Sheppard. During the eighteenth century it became the largest city in the western world.

Situated some five miles or so north of the City, it would be several centuries before Hornsey and Muswell Hill were to be seriously affected by London's territorial and demographic expansion. Muswell Hill farm had originated in an undeveloped wooded area. In 1370 over half the parish of Hornsey was forested, with the slow growth of cultivation centred around Crouch End. Much of the manorial lord's desmense wood was reserved for the bishop who fenced his park at Highgate and kept his hunting rights until 1660. Outside of Highgate, the most populous settlement in the parish, only about 60 or so houses existed, with a population of about 500. In 1647 a quarter of the parish was still wooded. Out of its 3,000 acres some 600 were common land. It was only in the seventeenth and eighteenth centuries that woodland clearance gathered pace. Population increased because of the increase in private estates, with an influx of people to serve them. Muswell Hill was to be affected by this change as estates began to be established there.

After the Dissolution several gentlemen, and their families in succession, held the former farm. These included John Avery, William Burnell, William Cowper, Thomas Golding and a London merchant tailor, John Goodwyn, after whom present day Goodwyns Vale was named. From 1554 part ownership of the property began to be held by the Rowe family when the reserved rent and other property were bought by Thomas Rowe, believed to be Sir Thomas Rowe, lord mayor of London 1568-69. The Rowe or Roe family, which was to include three Lord Mayors of London and Sir Thomas Roe, a notable courtier and explorer, had extensive land holdings not only in Muswell Hill, Hornsey, Finchley and Clerkenwell, but also in Kent where the family had originated. The mansion on the site (according to John Norden, with his reference to 'where Alderman Roe has now erected a proper house') was leased in 1601 to Bartholomew Matthewson. It is recorded as 'Mattysons' on the 1619 map of the manor of Tottenham made for the Earl of Dorset, lord of Tottenham manor. On this Dorset map it stands outside his manor, and is marked 'Mattysons Sr. Julius Caesar', after the occupant.

Sir Julius Caesar is the first known courtly resident at Muswell Hill. The name, unusual in England, refers to his Italian origin. His father was Adelmare Caesar (d.1569), a native of Padua who in 1558 became medical adviser to Queen Mary and subsequently to Queen Elizabeth I. Julius was born in this mansion, according to Clerkenwell historian William Pinks, and it was to be his country house. Sent to Oxford University at the age of 12, Julius trained for the law and became an eminent judge, as did his brother (Sir) Thomas Caesar. It was possibly from this mansion that Julius was called to the Earl of Arundel's house at nearby Highgate where his friend Sir Francis Bacon, courtier, lawyer, author of *Essays* and other works (and considered by some to be the real author of Shakespeare's plays) was ill from a chill, reputedly caught during an experiment in refrigeration, and where he died. Caesar was to become a member of parliament, Chancellor of the Exchequer in 1606, and Master of the Rolls (to James I) from 1614 to 1636, the year he died, aged 79. His tomb was placed in the chancel of St Helen, Bishopsgate.

Mattysons stood near the junction of Colney Hatch Lane with present day Muswell Road (in which a plaque marking the reputed site of the holy well is situated) as far as the Dorset map indicates. Standing there one can see a fine view towards the east. Busy shoppers passing this way have no indication that hereabouts was the site of a Tudor mansion. Memories tend to be more personal, of our own lives. I remember the corner because as Teresa and I pushed the pram with our second child up to the shops we met Alan Delafons, a colleague from my office, also pushing a pram; we discovered he lived in Dorchester Court, the corner block of flats.

The size of the mansion can be gauged from the returns for the Hearth Tax, levied from 1662 to 1689 on larger houses, with a tax of two shillings per hearth, collected at Michaelmas and on Lady Day. In 1664 Sir Thomas Rowe's house contained eighteen hearths. He demolished it in 1677, selling the building materials, but the Clerkenwell rate books for 1691-92 show that he still retained the site. Buildings said to be the grange of the Rowe's (that is an outlying granary or grain repository) were blown down in 1707. The site seems to have been part of farmland and to have had different occupiers till it was bought in 1826 by Thomas Bird who built a house called Wellfield on the southern boundary, about where Muswell Hill post office now stands. When Bird died the land was bought by the owner of adjacent Tottenham Wood Farm Thomas Rhodes, in 1834; his son, also Thomas, lived in Wellfield. Later it was occupied by Cornelius Nicholson who in his book *Scraps of History of a Northern Suburb of London* (1879) said he had found the foundations of the former nuns' chapel (though there appears no evidence to support this).

Chapter 3

Eighteenth Century Development

From Stuart times we can recognise Muswell Hill as a place of private residential estates, gradually increasing in number during the eighteenth century. Most of these survived until the end of the nineteenth century and afforded an ideal rural place of residence for their occupants who later were mainly to be drawn from professional and merchant backgrounds.

The origin of some estates was however upper class or aristocratic. John Warburton's 1725 map of Middlesex indicates seats owned by families with coats of arms and three are to be found at Muswell Hill, two on the side of the hill itself and the third in the angle between Colney Hatch Lane and the road towards Highgate. The house nearer the top of Muswell Hill, later known as Bath House, and the one at the south west end of Colney Hatch Lane, later known as The Limes both appear to have been in the ownership of the Rowe family, and to pass into that of the Pulteney family, Earls of Bath early in the eighteenth century.

I have traced some of the history of the estate known as The Limes in *People and Places: Lost Estates in Highgate, Hornsey and Wood Green*, edited by Joan Schwitzer and published in 1996 by the Hornsey Historical Society, and it is unnecessary to repeat that chapter here. Suffice it to say that the foundation of the estate probably occurred in the seventeenth century and to have been created by Sir Thomas Rowe (1641-1696) who provided in his will as follows:

'Whereas Muswell Hill is now double the value of what it once was when my father left it to me and whereas I have bought one house of my sister Mary and built a new house on the common, whereby the copyhold estate is much increased, I do therefore order that my wife enjoy her joynture and that my son Thomas Rowe do have all the rest of the estate being around £220 a year. After decease of my wife I give him the whole estate at Muswell Hill, hoping he will be a good husband and leave this to his (heir) and I with great (deal) of paine and care have preserved it for him'.

As waste or common usually lay each side of medieval roads I have speculated that Rowe built his house on a strip of common land at the end of the road from Highgate, where it joins Colney Hatch Lane. The house stood opposite what was Muswell Hill Common (mentioned earlier) but no map indicates a house on that common at this period. Indeed the common was the site of a bowling green created by Thomas Rowe which probably stood where No. 188 Muswell Hill Broadway (Brocklehurst's furniture shop) stands today. Its existence can be dated back to 1663 when the court rolls recorded the grant to Rowe of:

'a parcel of the waste now enclosed for the recreation and accommodation of all the tenants of the said manor, and of the gentlemen who shall contribute to the work and expense of a Bowling Green, being made at a rent of four pence per annum'.

The reference in Rowe's will to 'copyhold' is a reminder that much local land remained theoretically at least in the ownership of the lord of the manor i.e. the bishop of London whose manorial rolls are now held in London's Guildhall Record Office. Conveyance of property was subject to an initial surrender of it to the lord who then granted it to the next occupants. The word 'copyhold' derives from manorial tenants showing their evidence of their title to land in the form of 'copies' of the relevant entries on the manorial court rolls. They were 'copyholders' and their tenure was 'copyhold' which over time became converted to common law tenure or freehold.

By the early eighteenth century the branch of the Rowe family holding land at Muswell Hill petered out. The estates, heavily encumbered, were sold under the will of Henry Guy who had acquired the rights of the co-heirs. Guy was a wealthy member of parliament and guardian to William Pulteney. In 1726 the Muswell Hill properties became Pulteney's who was to become Earl of Bath (The family is not to be confused with the Thynnes who became Marquises of Bath and reside at Longleat, Wiltshire). It would have been in the eighteenth century that the house on the east side of Muswell Hill (which may have been the house bought by Rowe from his sister) became known as Bath House. It acquired a reputation as a house of entertainment, and an anonymous 1776 *Description of the County of Middlesex* reported that 'Roe's noble mansion became the property of the Earl of Bath but was lately converted into a public house'.

The last member of the Pulteney family was Henrietta Laura, countess of Bath, on her death judged to be the richest woman in England. Henrietta died childless in 1808 and the Muswell Hill properties passed to William Harry Vane, earl of Darlington and later duke of Cleveland. In 1810 he sold them, the transactions recorded in the Hornsey manorial rolls. Bath House had by then become a school, known as Bath House Academy and was sold for £1,400 to Thomas Milroy of Lombard

Street. The adjacent Green Man went for £1,000 to James Hawkins, the occupant and victualler and the Limes estate was sold for £5,500 to a man called Abbott Kent.

The other house shewn on Warburton's map situated on Muswell Hill was just south of Bath House and was to become well known as The Grove. As Dr Schwitzer has shewn in *Lost Houses of Haringey* (1986) the property seems to date back to the seventeenth century with the name a reference to the surrounding well-wooded landscape; there is a mention of Muswell Hill-grove in the seventeenth century manorial rolls. This house was to have a distinguished aristocratic occupant when from 1769 it was leased as a summer residence by Topham Beauclerk, great grandson of Charles II by his liaison with Nell Gwynn. This occurred just after Beauclerk had married Diana Spencer (1734-1808), daughter of the second Duke of Marlborough after she had divorced the profligate second Lord Bolingbroke with whom she had had three children in an unhappy marriage. 'Lady Di' was a talented painter and her portrait by Sir Joshua Reynolds may be seen in nearby Kenwood House today. (Some names echo down over the centuries; 'Diana Spencer' has a poignant other meaning for us).

Enjoying wonderful views, the Grove was to have landscaped grounds and Lady Di doubtless painted here. Beauclerk was a mixture of scholar and rake. James Boswell wrote to a friend that *'Mr Johnson went with me to Beauclerc's villa, Beauclerc having been ill. It is delightful, just at Highgate. He has one of the most numerous and splendid private libraries that I ever saw. Greenhouses, hothouse, observatory, laboratory for chymical experiments – in short everything princely'.* These comments indicate that Beauclerk was a keen scientist and The Grove was ideal for the telescope, with an astronomer kept on the premises. Due to the renown of the estate, visitors had to be restricted through the purchase in advance of a ticket to view, sometimes to the annoyance of some who had hoped to just drop in. Dr Samuel Johnson was perhaps the most noted of the visitors to Muswell Hill and the main tree-lined walk through the estate (now part of Alexandra Park) is known as Dr Johnson's Walk. But other eminent visitors included Horace Walpole, the art patron; Joseph Banks, the botanist who sailed with Captain Cook; and John Wilkes, the radical member of Parliament for Middlesex.

Later successively occupied by John Porker, City banker, William Johnstone, stockbroker, and William Block, silk merchant, the estate was bought in 1863 to add to the newly opened Alexandra Park, with inaugural celebrations of the opening held in its grounds. The estate remains part of the park but the house was demolished when the 1873 branch railway to the Palace was being constructed.

Another early property, dating back even to Tudor times, was down the hill from The Grove and has become known as the Grove Lodge estate, a rare survivor today. It was owned by Christopher Fulkes, then by Sir Paul Paynter and then in 1705 by Sir George Downing, builder of Downing Street. In 1708 it was acquired by the Dickins family and remained with them, with Charles Scrase Dickins the owner in 1837. Subsequent owners were city attorney William Ashurst, jeweller George Attenborough who rebuilt the house in 1854 and surveyor John Abraham who died in 1912 but whose family continued to own the estate till in 1945 Colonel Abraham gave it to the Red Cross. It now belongs to Haringey council. It contains some unusual trees and is part of a conservation area.

3. Rookfield House, with Avenue House beyond it, photographed in the mid-nineteenth century.

4. The Elms in 1880, facing the site of the present day roundabout.

The lodge building at Muswell Hill roadside for Grove Lodge survives today but the similar one it faced across the road has gone. This was the entrance lodge for Avenue House, an estate developed in the 18th century perhaps through purchase of parish waste from Muswell Hill common. From 1847 Avenue House was occupied by Richard Clay, member of a printing family whose company operates today from Bungay, Suffolk. In the 23 acres it occupied on the south west side of the Hill stood Rookfield House and Lalla Rookh, the latter occupied for six months in 1817 by the poet Thomas Moore (1779-1852) after one of whose poems the house was named. The whole property was acquired in 1899 by developer William Jefferies Collins whose family were to build the Rookfield Estate over much of it.

Another house and estate, probably developed in the eighteenth century, stood above Bath House at the road junction and was known as The Elms. It faced across to The Limes, with the village pond at the road junction between them. It survived until 1900 when it was demolished so that Dukes Avenue could be laid out over its grounds. Warburton's map shows other properties as Muswell Hill curved into Colney Hatch Lane and these smaller properties included a few shops. St James's Lane contained not only cottages but by the end of the eighteenth century a small wooden public house called The Royal Oak.

Other estates were developed in the eighteenth century adjacent to the roads to Highgate and to Fortis Green. Going to the Broadway for shopping, perhaps across to Bond and White, I rarely walk down Muswell Hill Road, though lately I stop at its junction with Grand Avenue to see Teresa's memorial bench. The road falls away here and is still known as Muswell Rise but in the early eighteenth century it was called Brettle's Hill after a local landowner. John Brettle began building up property here with the acquisition of a field and then a piece of common, according to research by Dr F M W Draper. On June 4th 1747, Draper says, Brettle was admitted at the manor court to a share of a cottage and a parcel of waste belonging to a certain Agnes Duncan. The house established here was known as The Hall and Draper says it stood more or less where the telephone exchange was built in Grand Avenue. The 1873 Ordnance Survey map shows it standing in open land between Fortis Green Road and the northern edge of Highgate Wood (but part of the estate was sold to allow the building of the 1873 railway line to Alexandra Palace.)

The Hall was the Brettle family country residence for they also lived in Bedford Row in London. John Brettle was a lawyer who in 1758 was made Secretary to the Stamp Office which administered a parliamentary tax on legal documents (something which was an irritant to American colonials in the lead up to the American War of Independence). He was succeeded in the post by his son, also John Brettle who had married the daughter of Lord Hawley. The second John Brettle as well as being a Justice of the Peace was also a volunteer officer with the Middlesex Militia where he rose to be a lieutenant colonel and was known as Colonel Brettle. John Lloyd in his history of Highgate refers to a tradition that George III visited the Hall to inspect 'a magnificent cedar tree that then graced the grounds' (Muswell Hill was always distinguished by its trees). Lloyd also quotes the Memoirs of a Miss L M Hawkins which, whilst praising Colonel Brettle's honourable way of dealing, remarks upon his parsimony 'He had a town house which was not only to the last degree dirty, but his villa, on one of the most beautiful eminences north of London, was in a condition that would have deterred many from sleeping in it *even in a moderate breeze*. He and his lady, who was of the most grotesque appearance, but of the most lively good-humour, were at perfect ease with persons of particular distinction, and whose notice conferred honour'. Thus Brettle was another resident who had access to courtly circles but who enjoyed the rural peace of Muswell Hill. He was a governor of Highgate School.

Brettle died in April 1801 and his wife in December 1802. Miss Hawkins wrote *'He had passed the age of ninety and had been some time confined to his bed. A violent cough attended his gout, and a spasmodic fit seizing him whilst giving orders to his coachman for the payment of some bills, he expired with a canvas bag of cash in one hand and a rouleau of banknotes in the other.'*

Lloyd then recounts a story that a groom took a position at The Hall so that he could pursue his activities from there as a highwayman, which he confessed to Brettle whilst in his death cell at Newgate prison. During the eighteenth century Finchley Common beyond Coldfall Wood to the north, was a notorious place for robberies of travellers with highwaymen escaping into the woods. Lloyd says that 'the position of the old house, surrounded as it then was by the common lands, and in the immediate proximity of Gravel Pit and Coalfall Woods, would render it most desirable as an easy and safe retreat – and who would suspect the trusted groom of a resident householder to be a highway highwayman?'

To the north of The Hall was another property, established in the angle between Fortis Green and Fortis Green Road. This was Fortismere, with another house to its south called The Firs. According to Draper this was built up partly by the acquisition of parcels of village waste or common from the parish, with John Brettle and Michael Hodgson allowed in 1784 by the parish vestry to have *'part of the common on Fortress Green, Muswell Hill'*. *The money arising from the above Sales being paid into the hands of the Surveyor of Highways for the time being to be applyd towards mending the roads in this parish and in Case any overplus shall arise it is to be paid into the Hands of the overseers of the Poor for the use of the said Poor'*. According to Draper it was Hodgson who began to build the estate. It is shewn on Milne's 1800 map and on the 1816 Hornsey Enclosure Award map. Fortismere and The Firs were to survive till early in the twentieth century, and when Collins built over the land he commemorated them in road names. Fortismere contained a large mere or lake which in the late nineteenth century especially was a popular venue for ice skating when frozen. A surviving photo shows a boat being rowed on it, with a boat house indicated on the 1894 Ordnance Survey map and fish ponds marked.

Across the road from Fortismere stood Fortis House, its location identified by the remnant of its mid-nineteenth century coachhouse which is now No. 38 Princes Avenue. The corner garden here is the site of the lawn in front of the house in which stood a giant cedar tree; when urbanisation occurred the public garden was created in order to save the magnificent tree. Ownership of the contiguous Fortis House and The Limes estates was sometimes separate and sometimes the same. It was the acquisition of both of them in 1896 which was to allow the building of the new suburb of Muswell Hill by James Edmondson, as will be told later.

Another eighteenth century estate identified by Draper stood on the outer bend of St James's Lane where it turns toward Muswell Hill. Known as Kutzleben Hall it was named after Baron von Kutzleben, representative in this country of the Landgrave of Hesse-Kassel, a small German principality that existed in the days before Germany was united into one country. Kutzleben was in England from 1771 and in 1780 took an English wife who was the daughter of a baronet. The official name of the mansion according to Draper was 'My Lord's House in the Bushes', later known as St James's House. The front garden was enclosed from the waste, with parish agreement, in January 1787. Kutzleben resisted recall to Hesse-Kassel and died at Muswell Hill on 28th August 1798. St James's House was later divided into three and still stood in 1891.

These eighteenth century estates shaped Muswell Hill round the old road system and with its few cottages and shops made up a rural hamlet of no great significance in itself, being seen as an appendage of the much more important village of Highgate with its chapel of ease. The estates were no more than a few acres in extent and were regarded as country residences, with ornamental gardens built around the house, avenues of trees, and the rest grassland, consisting of pasture, grazed by horses, sheep or cattle and meadows used for hay making, and the whole serviced by grooms and gardeners and indoor servants. A profusion of mature trees aided the sense of seclusion.

Farms also existed locally. Opposite The Hall was Upton Farm which, when it was bought in 1885 by the Imperial Property Investment Company, consisted of 42 acres, bounded by Muswell Hill Road, St James's Lane and Churchyard Bottom Wood (the old name for Queens Wood), and on the east stretched nearly to Park Road. There a medieval ecclesiastical demense farm of the Bishop of London called Rowledge still existed, some of it still preserved as open land today as Crouch End Playing Fields. The fields of Upton Farm are all built over, with Collins laying out Church Crescent at the northern end.

5. Upton Farm which stood in Muswell Hill Road opposite the site of present day Woodside Avenue.

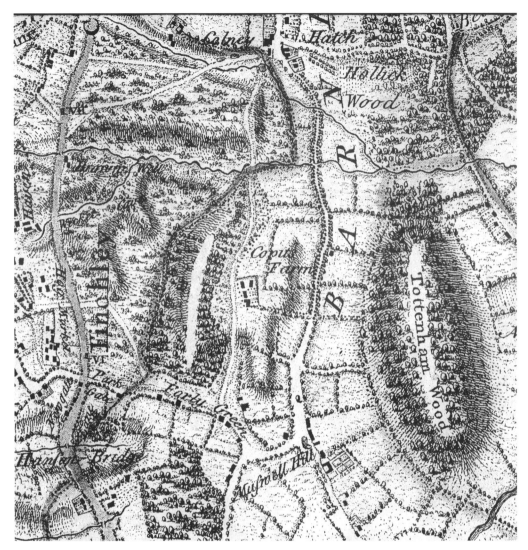

6. John Rocque's 1754 map of Middlesex showing Muswell Hill. Tottenham Wood was to become the site of Alexandra Park.

Coppetts farm in Coppetts Road (with its farmhouse dating from 1670) was used mainly for dairy work. East of it in Colney Hatch Lane, but in the parish of Friern Barnet, was Muswell Hill farm, owned early in the nineteenth century by Alderman Sir William Curtis. But the major farm near Muswell Hill was Tottenham Wood Farm, where Alexandra Park now is. Its name derived from the wood, which still survived as a remnant of the ancient Middlesex Forest when Rocque compiled his 1754 map of Middlesex. But when the lord of Tottenham manor put it up for auction with other lands in 1789 it was described as cleared, all but 11 acres. It was bought for farming by a Londoner, a Mr Mitchell.

Local farmland tended to be meadow or pasture but Tottenham Wood Farm had many arable fields in 1800, according to Milne's land utilisation map. But when Mitchell was succeeded by Thomas Rhodes this changed as Rhodes extended his holdings and aimed to have one thousand cows. According to G B G Bull's introduction to the London Topographical Society's edition of Milne's map, our zone of Middlesex was in the main devoted to hay-making, whereas other zones were devoted to market gardening, clay pits and cattle pasture. All revolved around the London market which continued to grow, with hay constantly needed to feed the horses which powered transport.

Thus during the eighteenth century a pattern of land occupation, dominated by a clutch of private estates and farms was consolidated, and lasted until nearly the end of the nineteenth century. As has been indicated the principal Muswell Hill properties came to be Bath House, The Limes, The Elms, The Grove, Grove Lodge, Avenue House (with Rookfield), The Hall, Upton Farm, Fortismere, The Firs, Fortis House and, further out, Coppetts Farm and Tottenham Wood Farm.

A similar pattern of estates existed across the rest of Hornsey parish. Between Muswell Hill and Hornsey village was the Priory estate. In Hornsey village were Campsbourne, the Grove House estate and the glebe land of the church. In Crouch End were Old Crouch Hall, Crouch Hall, Topsfield Hall and other properties. At Stroud Green was Stapleton Hall, the centre of a large farm. In Highgate a more urban landscape existed but it was dominated by some large houses and estates outside the village, particularly Kenwood and Holly Lodge.

For this rural parish of local landowners and villagers the Hornsey vestry was to become the centre of local government. In his comprehensive account of this vestry in *Hornsey Historical Society Bulletin No. 28* (1987), Richard Samways traced the main history of vestries, arguing that they emerged around the parish minister who had always been concerned with the plight of the poor and (with churchwarden help) had been responsible for the upkeep of the church fabric. Across the country from 1555 onwards surveyors of highways for each parish began to appear, says Samways, charged with maintaining local roads. From 1572 there were overseers of the poor not only to manage them but to collect parish alms from them. The nucleus of parish government was constituted in minister, churchwardens, overseers and highway surveyors, to which later was added the parish constable.

From the early sixteenth century vestry meetings are to be found in English records though the date of the first record of Hornsey vestry that appears to have survived is 1688. Meetings were attended by local residents, often the 'principal inhabitants' who paid church rates to maintain the church fabric. In 1601 the Poor Law Act introduced poor rates, that is local taxes specifically for expenditure on the poor. These were followed in 1654 by highway rates, with parish ratepayers having the right to attend vestry meetings. Both ecclesiastical and civil functions were dealt with, a practice which was to continue through the nineteenth century. As the vestry grew in importance so the manor court and other organs of local government declined.

The minutes for Hornsey vestry, under which Muswell Hill came, are now held in the London Metropolitan Archive with those for the years 1835 to 1867 held in Bruce

Castle. Up to the mid-nineteenth century they relate to a rural parish which had only about 230 houses in 1700 and no more than about 700 in 1800. Highgate was the most populous part and business was divided between Hornsey Side and Highgate Side, with two churchwardens, two overseers of the poor (whose names had to be ratified by two local Justices of the Peace), two highway surveyors and two constables (also appointed by JPs). A paid vestry clerk organised vestry meetings and kept the minutes. From 1774 there was a beadle (who received a new hat and coat every three years) who supervised the workhouse poor and kept order in church and in the village on Sundays. The churchwardens, highway surveyors, overseers and constables were unpaid local people who often sought to avoid being appointed, especially as it might mean their being out of pocket.

Hornsey vestry meetings were usually held on Sundays, either at the church or at a local public house such as The Three Compasses. In the eighteenth century these meetings do not appear to have been attended by the rector. Apart from the officers only about eleven local residents attended on average, even though there were at least 230 households. No analysis has been made of the people who attended but these tended to be the local gentry rather than the agricultural and other workers who made up the majority of the inhabitants (apart from a few shopkeepers).

Most of the parish business was concerned with the poor, with the assessment of individuals' rate liability and with its collection, the 1601 Poor Law Act having given vestries authority to levy this tax. Rates increased greatly in the eighteenth century. By 1743 the parish had a workhouse in Hornsey High Street administered by a master and a mistress; the young were apprenticed out to tradesmen and craftsmen.

Apart from parish vestries in the maintenance of law and order there existed throughout the country Justices of the Peace, who played an important role in the administration of local justice. Begun in medieval times as a royal appointment, they provided in later centuries valuable unpaid service, not only having jurisdiction over many indictable offences but also having responsibilities such as the licensing of alehouses and, as we have seen, the appointment of parish officers, and control over county police and county rates. The post of JP still continues, with different functions, to this day.

As far as parliamentary representation was concerned, Hornsey (and with it Muswell Hill) had no separate representation as a constituency until 1885, but freeholders voted for the two representatives which the county of Middlesex elected, with the polling place at Brentford. Parliamentary representation had begun in 1282 when knights of the shire represented the counties; Middlesex representatives had included Sir Roger Cholmely, founder of Highgate school who sat in 1554 and Francis Bacon in 1592.

By the eighteenth century the franchise was more democratic. Londoners living in Middlesex were often opposed to the government and perhaps the greatest expression of their rebelliousness was their election of John Wilkes as a member for Middlesex in 1768. Prosecuted by the government and outlawed for libel, he was expelled from the Commons in 1769 but returned, unopposed, by Middlesex electors in an election declared void; this was followed by another election in which he was again voted in by the electors. 'Wilkes and Liberty' became a popular call. In 1771 Wilkes was elected sheriff of London and Middlesex and was Lord Mayor of London in 1774, the year he finally again entered Parliament, having been returned for Middlesex unopposed.

What part if any Muswell Hill residents and landowners played in this political battle cannot easily be ascertained. We do know however that John Wilkes was a visitor to The Grove during Topham Beauclerk's tenancy. Born in 1725, the son of a Clerkenwell distiller and married for a while to an heiress, Wilkes died in 1797, one of his achievements being the press's right to publish parliamentary reports through his having used his position as a city magistrate to protect reporters.

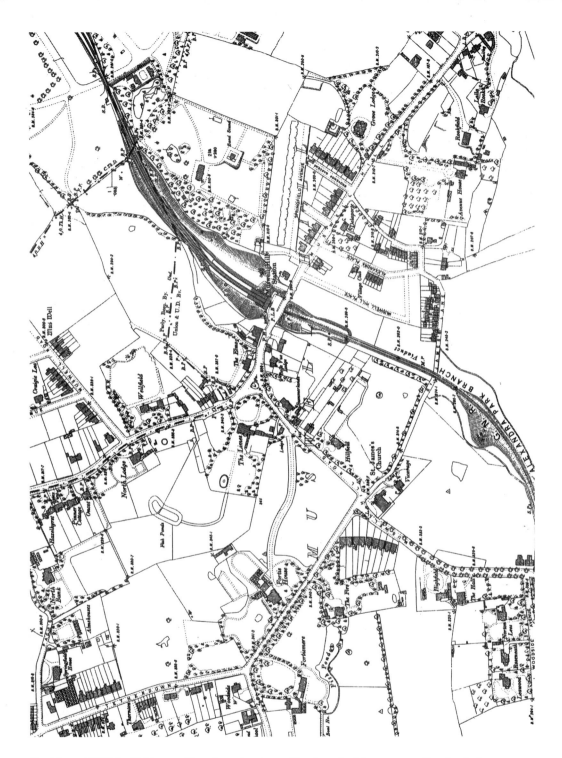

7. Muswell Hill in 1894 was still a place dominated by detached houses standing in their own grounds, as the OS map shows.

Chapter 4

The Last Rural Century

Muswell Hill in the nineteenth century remained a rural area topographically dominated by the private estates, the few farms and the early road system. By 1891 its population was still less than a thousand, even though the century had witnessed a gradual increase in the number of detached villas on smaller sites, and an increase in cottages and other dwellings for those who supported the larger houses with necessary services.

Muswell Hill gained a church in 1842, a church school in 1850, saw the arrival of Alexandra Park and Palace in the 1860s and gained a railway station in 1873. But the hamlet turned village did not succumb to the developer until 1896, despite three attempts to sell estates for this purpose in 1865, 1880 and 1885. It remained a delightful rural enclave, full of mature trees and fine views, with estates now occupied by business and professional families rather than by those with courtly or aristocratic connections. This rural seclusion was maintained whilst the rest of the old parish of Hornsey changed, from the late 1860s onwards, into a new conurbation which by 1903, with a population of over 72,000 had become a borough. By then of course the builders were well under way in constructing an Edwardian suburb of distinction in place of the rural scene on the heights of Muswell Hill.

The physical attractiveness of Muswell Hill as a place was recorded by travel writers such as J Norris Brewer in 1816 and John Hassell in 1817, the latter referring to it as:

'a little paradise.....clothed with the richest verdue and encircled with a redundance of wood (which)....will captivate and delight the admirers of landscape scenery on this hill'.

The quality of village life in the 1830s was remembered by the philosopher Frederic Harrison (1831-1923) who spent his first years in a house on the crest of the hill called Belle Vue Lodge and who was to write:

'On our Muswell Hill we knew the story and ailments of every villager; and I well recall the Quaker family of a small baker opposite and how their wisdom was called for in remedies and suggestions when one of my brothers scalded his chest with a mug of hot gruel and when another was thought to have swallowed a copper penny. There was no doctor within easy call, and the village was its own apothecary and nurse'.

'A few inhabitants who, like my father had daily business in the city went and came in the four-horse coach, the departure and arrival of which was the stirring incident in the life of Muswell Village.....I led her (a nurse) down to the lawn to behold from afar the towers and smoke of London gathered round the dome of St Paul's, as of some mighty and mystic world which it was our privilege to gaze upon and wonder at'.

Speaking personally, the view from the top of Hillfield Park, off the Broadway, fills me with the same sense of wonder as I gaze over London; it is one of Muswell Hill's greatest sights.

Landowning changes occurred early in the nineteenth century when the commons passed into private ownership. As the land remained largely unbuilt upon afterwards Muswell Hill's appearance did not dramatically change. Hornsey Enclosure Act was passed in 1813, with the Award operative from 1816. A similar Act had been passed for neighbouring Finchley parish in 1811. These parliamentary private acts were part of a national movement to develop common and waste lands, ostensibly to extend agricultural output as the population grew and industry developed. Between 1760 and 1844 there were about 4,000 such private acts allowing enclosure of the commons, affecting some six million acres.

In the case of Hornsey, commissioners were appointed to distribute common land throughout the parish and the accompanying map to the award of 1816, with numbered plots and associated Index, shows the distribution of land to individuals and others. The bishop of London, as lord of the manor, received 30 acres, the prebendary of Brownswood, landowner in the south of the parish 24 acres, the Rector of Hornsey 46½ acres and the rest went to copyholders, apart from a comparatively small amount collectively to the poor, 12½ acres at Irish corner in the north of the parish abutting Friern Barnet and a tiny 'allotments' of land next to woodland at Highgate.

Loss of the commons to private landowners under this Act meant that cottagers could no longer graze their animals as before. The essence of the process nationally was to be summed up in a satirical verse:

'The Law locks up the man or woman
Who steals the goose from the Common,
But lets the greater robber loose
Who steals the Common from the goose' .

Losses in the London area, as more building took place, was to mean a lack of open space for the poor living in crowded dwellings, a factor which helped lead to the provision of public parks, such as Victoria Park. Perhaps nationally this allocation of land made some contribution to agriculture but in Middlesex it provided more opportunities during the nineteenth century for Victorian residential estates to be developed.

8. Essex Lodge in Colney Hatch Lane, dating from the early nineteenth century, survived until circa 1960 till replaced by a block of flats.

9. North Bank in Pages Lane is a rare surviving nineteenth century house and estate.

Common land survived in Hornsey High Street, reputedly to preserve the rural look of Hornsey village; the grassed remnants can be seen today in front of the Great Northern Railway Tavern and at the other end opposite Middle Lane. But in Muswell Hill the whole common was to pass into private ownership, including that between St James's Lane and the hill, and Hornsey common on the west side of present day Tetherdown. Fortunately both remained largely unbuilt upon.

New properties not marked on the 1816 Hornsey Enclosure Award map are to be found on the first large-scale Ordnance Survey map of the area in 1865. In Colney Hatch Lane Wellfield is on the east side and nearly opposite on the west side is North Lodge, carved out of The Limes estate to provide a separate family home for the daughter of The Limes owner, Richard Marshall, by 1838. (Woodberry Crescent was built over this estate by Edmondson in Edwardian times). North of this property begins a line of detached villas which eventually were to stretch along the west side beyond Pages Lane almost as far as today's Barnards Hill. Only Nos 3, 5 and 7 now remain, in modified form, but representing some of the oldest domestic houses in Muswell Hill.

In Pages Lane, by 1865, there was an estate called The Hermitage where North Bank now is. Adjacent to it, where the block of flats called Whitehall Court was built in 1937, were the almshouses for five poor persons which Madame Uzcielli had provided in 1861. Standing behind Whitehall Court in the grounds of North Bank would have been the tall chestnut tree estimated recently by a scientist to date from the seventeenth century, described as the oldest living thing in Muswell Hill. West of the almshouses in 1865 stood another house called Springfield. It was to be taken over in 1907 by an order of French nuns to be converted into a convent with a private school.

No other properties are recorded in this area except in Tatterdown Lane (Tetherdown) where opposite the end of Pages Lane stood Muswell Lodge which in 1896 was to be the scene of a notorious murder (to be described later). At the southern end of Tetherdown, on the corner with Fortis Green, stood an estate called Woodside, backing onto Coldfall Wood; this was replaced in the 1920s by a Collins block of flats of the same name; opposite it was a property called Fortis Cottage. Elsewhere in Muswell Hill a parsonage had been built in St James's Lane just below the church (it was replaced by the present vicarage in 1915) and south of Grove Lodge now stood Rutland Villa in its own grounds with three more detached houses south of it (where flats now stand).

The map also indicates the housing, which was of a less affluent kind, which had developed from earlier origins along St James's Lane. By 1851 there were already 58 houses there, 16 forming alleys at the foot of the hill. Most of these were swept away in the 1920s but Vale Cottage survives. Similar development was going on along Fortis Green where timber cottages built along the southern edge of Coldfall Wood were supplemented by rows of small houses. Some of these survive. But property development on a more affluent level for Fortis Green was put under way in 1852 by the National Freehold Land Society which laid out Eastern, Southern and Western Roads as an intended Harwell Park Estate; this was only slowly built up. Nearby was the brewery in Fortis Green (on the site now occupied by the police station) with its own pub which served the needs of Great North Road travellers and others.

10. The first St James's church photographed in 1888. It was replaced by 1902 by the present church by which time the wooden palings had been replaced by shopping parades.

11. St James's Lane in 1888 crossed by the viaduct built for the 1873 branch line to Alexandra Palace.

The increasing parish population caused the rector of Hornsey, Richard Harvey, incumbent from 1829 till 1881, to promote the establishment of new Anglican churches, including St James's, Muswell Hill. By 1851 there were some 795 people living in 165 separate dwellings north of St James's Lane. A new church was to save them having to travel each Sunday, either to Hornsey village or to the chapel at Highgate in order to worship. The site chosen was at the top of St James's Lane, donated by local landowner Henry Warner who lived at The Priory, near the foot of Muswell Hill. The new church was designed by architect Samuel Angell and consecrated in 1842. Its tower, with clock and wooden spire, and later a mantle of ivy, became a notable feature at the road junction, standing among open fields. Extended in 1874 it was to serve Muswell Hill until the end of the nineteenth century when structural problems and the vastly expanding population caused the present much larger St James's church to be built; the clock made in 1843 for the old church was retained for the new tower.

With the building of the church Muswell Hill was no longer classified a hamlet but as a village. But it still remained an isolated hill-top settlement among verdant trees. As well as a church it also gained a church school. This was the era before state schools when provision for education was made (aided from the 1830s onwards by government funding) through the churches and chapels, either Church of England which built 'National' schools, or nonconformist which built 'British' schools.

A National school was opened in 1850 in Fortis Green (on the site occupied since 1969 by Charles Clore House, near Tetherdown). Designed by notable architect Anthony Salvin who designed villas for his brother-in-law and himself in Fortis Green and who also designed the National Schools in East Finchley (East End Road) and Highgate (North Road) it was first intended for infants before their going on to the National School in Hornsey, but soon catered for older girls, then older boys. By 1870 St James's National School was to take one hundred of Muswell Hill's 164 children aged between five and thirteen (whilst Hornsey National School only took 21). Enlargements of the building on the same site continued in later years. From 1931 it was a voluntary aided primary school, moving to Woodside Avenue in 1968. The old buildings were demolished in the following year.

The 1851 population census, the figures from which were analyzed by Jean Corker for a Middlesex Polytechnic thesis, showed that Muswell Hill had a higher proportion of professional, merchant and landowning class people than nearby but more agricultural Hornsey village. The census includes for Muswell Hill an attorney, bookseller, barrister, gold dealer, customs officer, printer, solicitor, silversmith and jeweller as well as merchants, dealers and manufacturers, in all making up over thirty per cent of the population. Some forty four per cent she classes as unskilled labour, including agricultural workers, gardeners, grooms, dairymen and the like; the remainder were the skilled, semi-skilled, lower professionals and domestic servants.

Who were these professional, merchant and landowning people occupying small landed estates in Muswell Hill? Some names may be picked out, such as Dr Protheroe Smith (1809-80) who occupied The Elms from the middle of the nineteenth century, though it must be remembered that he, like other Muswell Hill people of his class, would also have a town house. He would have needed a London base for he was a West End physician who had numbered Lord Palmerston among his patients. Smith specialised in women's diseases and set up the first women's hospital in the world in Red Lion Square (later in Soho Square). He pioneered the use of chloroform in childbirth.

Dr Protheroe Smith's concern with hygiene caused him to have Muswell Hill's village pond removed in 1858 (it was situated where the roundabout is now) and replaced by a tank with tap and pump. Wells provided the water supply for the large houses, with villagers taking water from Muswell Hill well. Small houses in St James's Lane depended upon a private well at The Priory. (Evidence at an 1860s railway line enquiry referred to women using yokes to carry buckets of water from Muswell Hill well).

Barrister William Manson lived in Bath House, which had been divided into three separate houses by 1860, with Manson living in the centre one. Manson was involved in a local action when the younger Thomas Rhodes attempted to stop people coming onto Tottenham Wood farmland to use the Muswell Hill well. He was defeated in 1862 in the case of Howell v. Rhodes, and the well continued to be used by local inhabitants, the path to it becoming the line of Muswell Road, laid out in the 1880s. William Manson's son Frederic Manson was to reside in Wellfield (built by the 1830s by Thomas Bird) after the younger Thomas Rhodes had left it (he died comparatively young) and was also to be the owner of the adjacent property, The Elms.

Another lawyer of wider renown was William Henry Ashurst (1792-1855) who resided at Grove Lodge from 1839 and had radical beliefs. A solicitor, he had refused to pay taxes until the 1832 Reform Bill was passed. He was an under-sheriff of London and was friendly with Rowland Hill, whose family opened a pioneering school in Bruce Castle, Tottenham, and helped him with the development of his penny postage innovation of 1840. Ashurst was a founder of the Society of Friends of Italy and as such often had as a guest at Muswell Hill the famous Italian patriot Giuseppe Mazzini (1805-72) who was banished from Italy and lived in London from 1836 to 1848.

Ashurst's daughter (later Madame Venturi) recorded the rural isolation of Muswell Hill in 1846 when there was only one omnibus and the Finchley coach with four horses once a day only each way, which afforded he sole means of transport. The editor of Mazzini's *Letters to an English Family* which Dr Draper quotes, wrote that:

'Muswell Hill, a village on the Hornsey side, was not at that time very accessible. By night no help could be obtained from rail or stage, and cabs being too expensive for most of the habitues, it was customary for the friends who had enjoyed Mr Ashurst's hospitality to assemble in the porch at about half-past ten and journey together on foot as far as the Angel, Islington, where cabs and omnibuses were available'.

Both Ashurst and his successor at Grove Lodge, the jeweller George Attenborough (who rebuilt the house in 1854) would have known the family living on the estate across the road. This was Avenue House, occupied from 1847 by Richard Clay (1789-1877) who had a successful printing business in the City on Bread Street Hill and who had previously lived at Highbury. After his death Avenue House continued in the occupation of the Clay family, with his son Richard running the firm. Charles, the eldest son of the family of six which survived infancy (four others did not) became the printer to the University of Cambridge.

Three of the Clay children married into local families at Hornsey and Highgate for a social life existed in the area, with parties bringing young people of similar status together. Less known to them, perhaps, would have been William Tegetmeier (1816-1912) of Hanoverian descent who was to become a naturalist and prolific journalist and author. He did research work on bees, using hives in his front garden, which was useful to Charles Darwin in compiling his *On the Origin of Species*. Tegetmeier is also credited with instigating international pigeon racing, with races taking place from Alexandra Palace. From 1858 he and his family lived on the perimeter of the Avenue House estate in an old weatherboard house, which still survives, in St James's Lane, and then in another house in the Lane. In 1868 Tegetmeier was to move to a 'better' house, Coldfall Lodge in Fortis Green, and could well have mingled with the well-to-do in their villa residences. A diary kept in 1872 by Marian Chambers, wife of an architect, who lived in a villa called St Martin's on Crouch Hill refers to a visit on Sunday 10th March by Mr Tegetmeier in the morning. 'His eyes very bad – dropsy in them'. (See *HHS Bulletin No. 22*).

Printing was the concern of the Clay family but other aspects of the book trade concerned residents of The Limes in the nineteenth century, details of which I give in *People and Places*. In sequence the occupants of this estate had been Jose de Bernales, a Spanish merchant who had extended his land ownings in 1816 but who had subsequently gone bankrupt, resided in a debtors' prison and had died soon after his release in 1825; Gurney, a shorthand writer; Richard Marshall (1789-1863) of the book wholesaling firm Simpkin, Marshall, two of whose grand-daughters were to marry into the Clay family; and from 1867 Charles Edward Mudie, founder and owner of Mudies Circulating Library which loaned books across the world. Mudie leased The Limes from his neighbour James Hall Renton, a stockbroker, and before that from the Somes ship-owning family who resided at Fortismere with Samuel Somes later becoming a merchant banker, showing that finance as well as the book trade was represented at Muswell Hill.

Close connections with the creative worlds of the arts in Victorian London were, however, forged at a house lying between Muswell Hill and Highgate called Woodlands, its site now occupied by the road Woodland Rise. Jules Kosky has described it in his chapter in *People and Places*. Built around 1850 it was occupied from 1861 for fifteen years by the Lehmann family who entertained people like Charles Dickens, Wilkie Collins, Edwin Landseer, Sir Charles Hallé and others. Most frequent visitor was probably Wilkie Collins who stayed a The Woodlands in 1869 in order to write a novel entitled *Man and Wife*. The Lehmanns also entertained their neighbours in Muswell Hill. Dr Draper records their including Mr Bockett who lived at The Firs in Fortis Green Road at a dinner party which contained an eccentric guest called Chorley, writer for a magazine called the *Athenaeum*. Draper also records that two nieces of Mr Bockett married at Muswell Hill the brothers of Gerard Manley Hopkins in 1872 and 1873 (the Hopkins family then living at Hampstead). Also among this circle was the poet Coventry Patmore, who lived at a Fortis Green house called Highwood Lodge, between Eastern and Western Roads.

How were the varying needs of these gentry, with their indoor and outdoor servants, met? Produce would have been provided by kitchen gardens, orchards, grazing cows and hens. Furnishings would have been delivered by department stores such as Jones Brothers of Holloway, or those in the West End. In addition the village was visited daily by horse-drawn carts bringing supplies, operated by shopkeepers in both Hornsey and Highgate villages.

Muswell Hill is said to have had only four shops, near the top of the hill. The 1865 Ordnance Survey map indicates that the post office was next to the Green Man; this would be the building now occupied by a restaurant called Café Loco (previously Chicago 20s); this seems to be a late eighteenth century building, thus making it one of the earliest surviving buildings in Muswell Hill, now sandwiched between the rebuilt public house and the Exchange, the row of shops which Edmondson built in 1900. By 1890 these premises were described as a general shop, the post office having moved round the corner, to be kept by the Misses Archer.

Opposite the Green Man, and jutting onto the pavement is a building also probably of eighteenth century origin, which has been known as the White House. In the middle of the nineteenth century it was in use as a butcher's, opening twice a week. Later it became a confectioner's and tobacconist's, until occupied by Mr G H Smith who carried on a large house-decorating business. His father, Benjamin Smith, lived in Pages Lane and employed Charles White who was to be one of the founders in 1880 of the still-thriving local firm of Bond and White. The White House has a special importance for me as it is where Teresa and I negotiated the purchase in 1954 of our house in Alexandra Park. It was then occupied by Alfred Slinn's estate agency and when he took over in 1938 Slinn promised to preserve the old beams (I can't remember them). Slinn's agency has long gone but in recent years the building has again been occupied by another estate agency. A second shop stands next door.

Castle Villas in Colney Hatch Lane can still be discerned today, matching a sketch of them in Pinks's *History of Clerkenwell*; but their former front gardens are occupied by single storey shops. Castle Villas stood here by 1865, as the map shows. South of them was Boundary House, a property so named because it stood on the boundary of Clerkenwell Detached with Hornsey. Those beating the bounds of Clerkenwell would go through the house (this procession was the old way of asserting boundaries, especially to be noted by younger people). George Smith used the site just north of Castle Villas as his builder's yard; this has become the site of Woolworth's.

12. Castle Villas (left) on the east side of Colney Hatch Lane still survive, their front gardens occupied by single storey shops.

St James's Lane residents were at one time able to buy some articles over the bar counter in The Royal Oak but by 1889 a row of eleven houses known as St James's Terrace had been built and the end one traded as a grocer. In sum therefore the small village of Muswell Hill had just a few shops and only two public houses. Neighbouring Fortis Green had about five shops and two more pubs.

The second half of the nineteenth century saw premature attempts to develop Muswell Hill with housing. When in November 1863 Richard Marshall the owner of The Limes estate died (his wife having died the year before), the estate was purchased soon after by the London and County Land Building Company for £10,000 from the Marshall estate trustees (which included his son). But when the land was put up for auction in lots (for building) in 1865 the whole estate was preserved by being bought by neighbouring gentry. The purchasers were the Somes (or Soames) family who lived at Fortismere. They were ship owners with Samuel Somes describing himself in 1881 as a merchant banker. By making this purchase they were able to keep their own estate within a rural setting. Muswell Hill remained untouched.

13. The Royal Oak in St James's Lane photographed in 1937. It was replaced in 1965 by a larger building.

Perhaps attention had been drawn to Muswell Hill at that time by the purchase in 1863 of Tottenham Wood Farm. In the ownership of Thomas Rhodes this had been extended to some 450 acres, stretching from Colney Hatch Lane east to the Great Northern Railway (this was the parish's first railway line, with a station at Hornsey village in 1850). Rhodes was great uncle to Cecil Rhodes who made his fortune in Africa. When Thomas Rhodes died in 1865 he had outlived his son and the family seemed intent on securing residential development of their land. This proposal seems to have been linked with the plan to open a private park with villas and to build an exhibition centre on the farm, in emulation of the Crystal Palace which by 1854 had been moved to a private park in Sydenham, south London after its triumphant debut as the world's first international exhibition building in Hyde Park in 1851.

The architect Owen Jones, closely associated with the Crystal Palace, in 1858 designed a huge glass building as a 'Palace of the People' at Muswell Hill but it was never built. In 1863 Alexandra Park was inaugurated on the farmland and from 1866 the first Alexandra Palace began to be erected, made of stone and brick from the dismantled 1862 international exhibition building in South Kensington. It opened in 1873 only to be burnt down sixteen days later. A second palace opened on the site in 1875. Spreading over nearly eight acres the building is an expression of Victorian grandeur if not conducive to aesthetic delight; it has been partly rebuilt after a disastrous fire in 1980 and is a listed building.

Muswell Hill was provided with a railway station as a result of this development which saw its success as dependent upon access by rail. A branch line was built from Highgate to the palace. Constructed 1871-72, the legacy of this line remains today in the magnificent seventeen-arch railway viaduct which crosses St James's Lane and which nowadays carries not railway tracks but the linear park known as the Parkland Walk. The station stood just below The Green Man. The passenger railway operated until 1954. The station may have stimulated the building of nearby Grosvenor Gardens and the laying out opposite of Muswell Hill Place and Alexandra Place (now Gardens) which were to be built up piecemeal. The Village Club in Alexandra Place was provided in 1888 by Alexander Manson in memory of his wife, Phoebe, 'who took a kind interest in the welfare of the working classes, especially in St James's Lane.' Muswell Hill's first council school for infants and juniors opened in 1913 in Alexandra Place (since demolished for housing).

Despite the 1873 railway station Muswell Hill was not then ready to become part of London's suburbia although development in the long term remained probable. Partly successful was house building on Clerkenwell Detached where the company owning the Alexandra Park estate (which stretched as far west as Colney Hatch Lane) gained parliamentary permission in 1880 to sell off 80 acres in an attempt to deal with their desperate financial situation. Muswell Road, Muswell Avenue and Middleton (now Coniston) Road were laid out by 1885 but the take-up of plots was slow. Partly this was due to complications over local authority services, especially disposal of sewage as this was an island of Clerkenwell, set apart; the situation was not fully resolved until 1900 when the area of Clerkenwell Detached was restored to Hornsey.

14. The first Alexandra Palace built circa 1866 was gutted by fire soon after its 1873 opening and replaced by the present building.

15. The large lake on the Fortismere estate was used for boating and when frozen for ice skating.

16. The 1873 railway station stood on Muswell Hill just below The Green Man and provided passenger services until 1954. It was later demolished.

17. The full splendour of the railway viaduct can no longer be seen due to the building of Muswell Hill Place in the foreground. This 1888 photograph shows the St James's Lane properties (left).

The Elms was seen as a property which might be developed when it was put up for auction in 1880; the freehold property with 11 acres was offered as 'Being also highly valuable for development as a Building Estate' with the accompanying map outlying a 'suggested new road'. This did not happen and the old, ivy covered , three-storey, nine-bedroom mansion stood facing the road junction for another 20 years. The concept was realised when James Edmondson demolished the house and laid out Dukes Avenue over the land.

Five years later development was also proposed for the 23 acres Avenue House estate, offered in July 1885 as being 'well adapted for the erection of superior residences and for residences of a smaller character'. No developer took it until bought by Collins in 1899.

Victorian villas continued to be added to the Muswell Hill landscape where sites were available. On land just north of the branch line to the Palace, where it crossed under Muswell Hill Road three were built. Norton Lees was erected in 1875 for Sheffield silversmith Harry Atkin who managed the London office and who named the villa after a Sheffield district. Roseneath and Lea Wood were built next to it, each of the three houses standing in 2½ acres. The cul-de-sac was to become Woodside Avenue. In 1927 all three were sold and became part of the St Luke's Hospital complex. Norton Lees in 1889 was the scene of an attempted armed robbery during which a member of the Atkin family was wounded. (The story is told by Jill Hetherington in detail in *Hornsey Historical Society Bulletin No. 31*).

Other development in the 1870s on a less grand scale took place in the Tetherdown area. Properties suitable for occupation by artisans, builders and others, who served the people living in detached villas were built on the corner of Pages Lane and Coppetts Road and were known as Tatterdown Place. This brick-built group of two storey cottages and small houses still survives.

Opposite them, just past the small shops now on the southern corner of Pages Lane, there was to be a convenient pub but this became instead Stanley Lodge, now numbered 80-82 Tetherdown and rebuilt. Till 1999 this was the only building in Muswell Hill to have a plaque to a resident. The poet and influential literary figure W E Henley (1849-1903) lived here from Easter 1896 for two years till, after an operation, he moved to the south coast. *'We are victims of the British Builder'* he wrote on arrival in his rented property, *'but the house shapes gallantly, all the same....The Bar (for instance) is already on the spot; and so are the Tap-Rooms – whence I write'*. When 23 Henley had had a foot amputated and R L Stevenson is said to have based Long John Silver upon him. Henley's most famous poem was *Invicta* with the lines *'My head is bloody but unbowed'* and *'I am the master of my fate, I am the captain of my soul'*. (Muswell Hill's other plaque is at 37 Curzon Road where lived Auguste Jaeger, the 'Nimrod' of Elgar's Enigma Variations, erected 1999 for The Elgar Society).

18. One of three surviving 1870s villas in Woodside Avenue, now incorporated into St Luke's Hospital.

19. Surviving 1870s cottages in Pages Lane.

Tetherdown developed in the late 1870s and 1880s on both sides of the road, smaller houses on the west (one with 1873 date stone) and on the east Bellvue villas (No 66/68) then three tall pairs with Gothic gables. Detached villas on the west side were Newport (occupied by the French nuns before moving to Springfield and still surviving in Haringey use), Blymill, now gone, and Thorntons which was absorbed into Tollington school when it was built in front of it.

Opposite St James's church a terrace of substantial houses with long gardens was built, probably in the 1880s. Two survive but the others were demolished in 1936 to allow the Odeon cinema complex to be built. A Victorian villa was built in the 1880s on the opposite side of St James's Lane from the church and called Hillfield, an appropriate name for the sloping land. Occupied by a scientist called William Barlow it had only a short life of about 15 years before Edmondson built Hillfield Park and other properties over it.

In sum this late Victorian building did not add up to very much and there was little difference in the size of the built environment between 1865 and 1894 as the first and second editions of the Ordnance Survey maps of those dates show. Muswell Hill continued as a place still dominated by villas and small estates with a fringe of poorer properties.

The scene elsewhere in Hornsey was no longer so rural in the second half of the nineteenth century as London stretched outwards. London expanded enormously in trade, manufacture and population, becoming the centre of a world-wide territorial empire and of world finance. One significant 'nineteenth century invention', as Donald J Olsen called it in his *Growth of Victorian London* was the purpose-built office-block of the 1830s which replaced the medieval tradition of merchants residing over their counting houses. This helped increase the dichotomy between place of residence and place of work on which London's expansion was based. This was facilitated by the development of mechanical forms of transport – train, bicycle, tram and bus – which enabled workers to travel cheaply and so live further out from their place of work than the distance they were willing to walk.

Gradual intrusion of terraced houses and estates into the fields around London, a complex process depending upon availability of land as well as transport, characterised the nineteenth century and in this context Muswell Hill was one of the last local areas to be affected. But it was something of which it was very much aware. A trade paper report of 1885, for example, wrote about Charles Mudie, the founder of the circulating library who lived in The Limes, as a sociable man and

'in the habit of giving high entertainments at his garden parties in the comfortable house on the top of Muswell Hill.....the Muswell Hill house is still a fine country residence, though there is now a railway station near, and bricks and mortar are filling the vacant green slopes which have been so dear to many generations of Londoners.'

These green slopes were elsewhere in Hornsey, with the parish beginning to be built over in the late 1860s, starting in the area of Hornsey Village. Crouch End began to emerge as an urbanised place in the 1880s following the urbanisation of Stroud Green and Finsbury Park in the 1870s. Neighbouring Wood Green, the other side of the railway was transformed from the 1880s by the building of the Noel Park and

Harringay estates. By the 1890s the Priory estate along Priory Road, and Muswell Hill itself, were the last major undeveloped areas in Hornsey. They survived almost to the end of the century.

The population figures for Hornsey show that the equivalent of a modern town was built amongst the rural settlements during the last quarter of the century. A modest population of 11,082 in 1861 was to rise steadily, the census figures pointing up the change: 19,357 in 1871, 37,078 in 1881, 61,097 in 1891, 72,056 in 1901.

Parish vestries in the nineteenth century could not deal with the problems arising from urbanisation, such as drainage. Various bodies, often with overlapping functions, were established under government acts to deal with them. Under the 1858 Local Government Act parishes could set up Local Boards of Health and despite a tendency to resist new developments Hornsey finally adopted the Act in 1867 and set up Hornsey Local Board of Health (the monogram LBH is still to be seen on street furniture, for example on a hydrant cover on the roundabout). Two years before an independent Board had been set up for South Hornsey where building was more advanced, and the area south of Seven Sisters Road became separate from Hornsey proper; in 1899 it was to be included in Stoke Newington local authority.

Hornsey Local Board became the effective authority, though two churchwardens and four overseers were still in post in 1891, looking after the church and liaising with the Edmonton Poor Law Union which after an important 1834 Act took over responsibility for the poor in several parishes. The Board had 15 members and met fortnightly, with committees for sewers, water and nuisance removal, for roads and works, and for finance. By 1891 it had the services of a clerk, accountant, solicitor, engineer and surveyor, medical officer of health, rate collectors, sanitary inspectors, building inspectors and road foreman. The offices were built in 1869 in Southwood Lane, Highgate and continued in use until Hornsey Town Hall was built in Crouch End Broadway in 1933-35.

Under parliamentary legislation the Local Board was replaced in 1894 by Hornsey Urban District Council (with HUDC on street furniture instead of HLB). Retiring chairman of the Board was H Reader Williams, a wine merchant and Liberal who lived at The Priory. In recognition of Williams's hard work, which included saving open spaces, the Clock Tower in Crouch End Broadway was erected by public subscription in his honour, with a medallion portrait on it. Unveiling was in 1895, two years before he died. In 1891 only one HLB member lived at Muswell Hill, Edward Upton who resided at The Chestnuts, one of several villas between Woodside Avenue and Fortis Green Road on Muswell Hill Road.

Parliamentary representation changed in 1885 when Hornsey became one of seven Middlesex Divisions returning members. In 1891 the MP was Henry Stephens of the Stephens Ink firm who lived at Church End, Finchley. The constituency at that time included Finchley, South Hornsey and some outvoters. In 1918 the municipal borough of Hornsey (created 1903 in place of the UDC) became a parliamentary borough always returning Unionist or Conservative members, until 1992 when a Labour MP, Barbara Roche, was elected. Mrs Roche became a junior minister in the Blair government and lived in Muswell Hill.

Chapter 5

The New Suburb
is Born

The year 1896 is one of the most significant in the later history of Muswell Hill. It began in February with a notorious murder. Mr Henry Smith, a 78 year old widower who lived in Muswell Lodge, Tetherdown (where Burlington Road is now) was found bound, gagged and very dead, despite his security precautions, which included a trip wire which could fire a gun, installed in his garden backing onto Coldfall Wood. The perpetrators of this unsuccessful burglary were traced through a lantern which they had left behind and within a few months they were brought to trial, convicted and hanged, the expression 'He done him in' being said to have been first used by one of them during the proceedings.

The case brought enormous public interest, as murders seem to do. The murder took place on 14th February 1896 and the local paper, the *Hornsey Journal* was to report that on Sunday, 16th February, some 15,000 to 20,000 people visited the neighbourhood of Muswell Lodge. The publicity brought to Muswell Hill by the murder led to its development, it used to be said. The truth is more prosaic. The area came to the attention of an important developer, James Edmondson.

> 'It was whilst out for a spin on his cycle that the natural beauties of Muswell Hill, and its advantages as a prospective suburb, first impressed him,' wrote William Cummins in his newspaper the Muswell Hill Record. '...Edmondson first took in hand the development of Muswell Hill as an up to date suburb by purchasing the estate occupied by The Limes and Fortis House, two fine mansions.'

20. Muswell Lodge in 1882 the scene of the famous 1896 murder of Henry Smith. Its Tetherdown site is now covered by Burlington Road.

21. A family photograph of James Edmondson, founder of present day Muswell Hill; he was a keen cyclist.

The 1894 Ordnance Survey map, published two years before (see page 34) shows these properties lying between Fortis Green Road and Colney Hatch Lane. During the nineteenth century the two estates were either separately owned or owned by the same person, as I have shown in my chapter in *People and Places*. When the Somes family purchased The Limes in 1865 to save it from development the adjacent Fortis House estate was already owned by James Hall Renton, born 1821 in Scotland, a successful stockbroker whose main residence was 39 Park Lane in the West End and whose son Leslie was to become Liberal MP for Gainsborough from 1906 to 1910. Renton used the park-like grounds as a stud farm.

Joseph and Samuel Somes leased The Limes in 1867 to Charles Edward Mudie, founder of a mammoth private lending library with premises in New Oxford Street storing several million books. At some date ownership of The Limes passed to Renton, for after Mudie left the house in 1887 (three years before his death, aged 72), Renton leased it to a civil engineer, William Lake, for a seven-year period expiring in September 1896. However, James Hall Renton died on 22nd January 1895 and in August of that year his heirs sold just under 30 acres, incuding The Limes, to local lawyer and landowner Frederick Manson (see page 41). In April 1896 Manson sold on the property to James Edmondson for £25,000.

Possession of land is the necessary key step before new housing can be built, and it was Edmondson's acquisition of this land, some 30 acres in the centre of the village, and comparatively flat, that allowed him to build a middle-class suburb. The mature trees began to come down and the old paling fencing to vanish. The impact on the occupants and owners of the surrounding private estates can be imagined. Their rural enclave was to go. They were willing to sell and Edmondson was able to buy Hillfield, The Elms, Wellfield and North Lodge to expand his area of building. His development aided other builders, in particular William Jefferies Collins, who expanded Edmondson's suburb, especially on the east and south sides, by building over Fortismere and The Firs and then acquiring Avenue House estate on the side of Muswell Hill.

James Edmondson was one of the early motorists but also a keen cyclist; a surviving family photograph shows him standing by a penny farthing bicycle and doubtless his cycling hobby helped him survey areas where it might be possible to build. The development of London's suburbs was carried out by many builders, some small scale, some like Edmondson on a much larger scale, and their names have often been forgotten. Firms like that of Edmondson, Collins and John Cathles Hill (who built much of Crouch End) transcended smaller builders who erected a few rows of houses before often becoming bankrupt. They were closer to the model of the gigantic firm of Thomas Cubitt who built Belgravia and Pimlico.

How did Edmondson's building firm originate? James's father, Isaac Edmondson was born in 1831 in Cumberland. Beginning life as a farmer, running a blacksmith's and undertaking building work, Isaac came to London to build and by 1891 was living in Green Lanes, Stoke Newington in a house called Woodberry Lake (Woodberry was the name James was to use for his own houses and which he gave to Woodberry Crescent, Muswell Hill). James was born in 1857 and had a sister born in 1869. He joined his father's firm which had become known as Messrs. I Edmondson and Son Ltd., operating from No. 8 The Broadway, Highbury Park. It was a private limited company from 1906. James married, and his wife Isabelle had three sons and one daughter. Two of the sons were killed in the 1914-18 war, one in the army, one in the navy, but the firm became James Edmondson & Son Ltd. The surviving son, Major Albert James Edmondson (1887-1959) became Conservative MP for Banbury and a junior government minister and was knighted in 1936. In 1945 he was enobled as 1st Baron Sanford. His son (born 1920) the Rev. John Edmondson DSC, succeeded to the title.

The Edmondson firm built extensively in north London, from Golders Green to Winchmore Hill, and as far afield as Westcliff-upon-Sea, in Essex. By 1885 they helped shape the look of Crouch End by building Topsfield Parade on the site of Topsfield Hall, with the Clock Tower built in front of it (constructed by a Highgate building firm). Keen observers will note that Topsfield Parade is the same in architectural terms as Queens Parade, Muswell Hill, built soon after (though the other Muswell Hill parades vary in appearance). Edmondson established a local office at 6 Station Parade after he had built it on the south west side of Colney Hatch Lane, and at No. 1 Queens Avenue, the house next to the library (I was sorry to see that alterations to the house in 1996 led to the removal of a large manhole cover with Edmondson's firm's name on it, the only one I knew about – perhaps there are others surviving?)

Ill health caused James Edmondson to move in 1923 at the age of 64 to West Overcliff, Bournemouth although without giving up his business interests. His house there was named Woodberry Lake. He died in June 1931 and is buried in Bournemouth Central Cemetery. The estate office continued in Queens Avenue until the late 1920s and the firm continued after the Second World War but was taken over and its records apparently exist no longer.

Edmondson wasted no time in submitting plans for development to Hornsey Urban District Council, proposing 19 dwelling houses and shops along Muswell Hill Road, to be called Queens Parade, 14 dwelling houses and shops along the west side of Colney Hatch Lane to be called Station Parade, and 55 houses in Queens Avenue, the major residential road of his new suburb, with stabling at the rear of the parades. He also designed Princes Avenue from Muswell Hill Road to Fortis Green Road. Plans were finally agreed by the council in October 1896, Edmondson having agreed to Fortis Green Road being 60 feet wide rather than 40 feet, and offering to contribute £1,000 towards making up the road and to construct the Tetherdown portion. 'That', thought Councillor José, 'was a very good arrangement indeed; he did not know that they had ever had such favourable terms before…'

Q. Ave not on 1895 OS Map

The width of Fortis Green Road was set in the days of horse transport, when the motor car had only just begun to be manufactured (the first British company formed was named the Great Horseless Carriage company) and the 1896 Highways Act had only just raised the speed limit to 14 miles per hour and dispensed with a man on foot carrying a red flag proceeding any powered vehicle on the road. So when we motor comfortably along Fortis Green Road, sometimes double parking our vehicles, we should give a thought to Hornsey UDC and to the generosity of Edmondson in 1896.

Another feature of Fortis Green Road that we owe to Edmondson is the small garden on the corner of Princes Avenue. Behind it still stands a remnant of Fortis House coach house. The old mansion stood here, and in front of it was the fine old cedar tree which people wanted preserved. Edmondson duly obliged and refrained from building Princes Avenue all the way to the corner and offering the council 'a piece of ground 50 feet nine inches by forty six feet', the condition being that the council 'will maintain the space as a public garden for ever'. Councillor Burt said 'this cedar was one of the finest in north London'. Old postcard views show it towering higher than the parades which Edmondson built in Fortis Green Road. It was finally removed in February 1918 when, having died, it was considered a safety hazard by Hornsey's Borough Engineer. Replacements of the tree have been made.

Queens Avenue was made 65 feet wide by Edmondson as his fine central residential thoroughfare, designed to attract upper middle class residents. As the decades passed some of these houses were considered too large and some have been combined to make hotels. (In 1999 there were four: Roseview and Raglan Hall on the north side and Queens and National on the south). Princes Avenue, was said later to be more fashionable, with at least one house having a butler. Today, despite some contemporary multi-occupancy the quality suburb has been maintained virtually intact.

A pertinent comment was made by the *Hornsey Journal* in September 1899:

'A decade ago Muswell Hill and neighbourhood was inhabited only by a few wealthy people but during the last two or three years miles of streets have been laid out, hundreds of houses have been erected and an innumerable number are now in the course of construction...Among all the newly built and unoccupied houses at Muswell Hill there is not one suitable for a working man'.

The comment was sparked off by the case of an evicted lamplighter who lived in a tent in a field. Other features were approved:

'A row of young lime trees have been planted either side of Queens Avenue...they are placed at intervals and taken in conjunction with the pretty villas, with their artistically arranged flower gardens in front, they should in a few years make this an exceedingly pleasant promenade and the most attractive thoroughfare in the district'.

A contemporary advertisement in 1899 by the Imperial Property Investment Company offers houses to be sold across Hornsey at prices from £325 to £2,000 or to be let at rents from £28 to £150.

22. Princes Parade, then Queens Parade on the left,and Victoria Parade, on the right, were built by Edmondson as the core of his new suburb.

23. The preservation of the cedar tree in front of what had been Fortis House led to the creation of the public garden on the corner of Fortis Green Road and Princes Avenue.

In 1899 Edmondson submitted plans for St James's Parade in Fortis Green Road with 20 shops with residential flats over, and for 38 dwelling houses in Hillfield Park which he had laid out over the estate occupied by William Barlow. He also put in plans for 14 sets of residential flats in St James's Lane with a bicycle house at the rear. A date stone at the foot of Hillfield Park, on the end wall gives the date 1901. Edmondson widened St James's Lane and built Victoria Parade from the lane along Muswell Hill Road, with a gap for Hillfield Park.

Each parade of shops and flats built by Edmondson around the perimeter of his Fortis House/The Limes estate was named and used as the postal address. These were in sequence Grand Parade and St James's Parade in Fortis Green Road, Princes Parade and Queens Parade in Muswell Hill Road (with Victoria Parade on the other side of the road) and Station Parade in Colney Hatch Lane, with Royal Parade opposite, north of the new sorting and post office which he built. These names remained in use until 1960 when Hornsey Borough Council decided that, with the growth in trade and motorised deliveries addresses there were difficult to identify so they abolished them and renumbered them as Muswell Hill Broadway. Previously 'Broadway' had been the name of the shops and premises between the Express Dairy (at the top of the hill) and Victoria Parade (by Hillfield Park). The names of the parades all disappeared except one plate for Station Parade which survived, mostly by being hidden under an advertisement hoarding at the time of the change, until it strangely disappeared in 1997. Muswell Hill Broadway is now numbered from No. 1 at Fortis Green Road to No. 353 at Woodberry Crescent on the one side and from No. 2 at St James's Lane to No. 522 at Muswell Road on the other. (Personally I have always found this confusing, especially as the shop numbers do not run in simple sequence as they have to take in the numbers for the residential flats above. I suspect that many would like the parade names restored and more simple shop numbering used.)

Queens Parade between Princes and Queens Avenue was the first to be built and on the second door on the right in Princes Avenue from the Broadway can be seen an 1897 date stone. This I always call Muswell Hill's birth certificate. In 1997 the first century was rightfully celebrated. The centenary was particularly a matter of pride for Martyn's, the family-owned provision shop (noted for its smell of grinding coffee) which has been in Queens Parade since it was built and which still continues as a favourite shop for local residents to visit.

Edmondson in 1899 also purchased The Elms and Wellfield estates, which lay in Clerkenwell Detached. In 1900 this came under the control of Hornsey as under an 1899 London Government Act boundaries could be adjusted and in October 1899 an Assistant Commissioner adjudicated that the 64.5 acres should go to Hornsey. In evidence at the enquiry 'Mr J. Edmondson said he had recently purchased a large freehold site at Muswell Hill and of the 20 acres 12 were in Clerkenwell Detached. The rental of the properties he intended erecting was from £80 to £100'. The Elms estate was only 11 acres so his purchase would have included Wellfield.

By this time both estates were owned by Frederic Manson, mentioned earlier. It is of interest that Wellfield was briefly occupied by Thomas Lipton, who had developed a huge grocery store chain and had become famous through his transatlantic yacht racing. Lipton moved to Ossidge Lane, Southgate. Purchase of the Wellfield estate

24. Hillfield Park properties cascade down the slope; beyond London fills the Thames valley landscape.

25. The former Presbyterian church, now converted into a pub, was once described as 'the nose on the face of Muswell Hill'.

meant that Edmondson's property extended to Muswell Road, laid out in the 1880s, where the well was situated. By this time the well was in a neglected state, with its iron canopy broken. Its exact location was disputed in later years, Alderman Goulding saying it was near Elms Avenue, others that it was just past the houses numbered 34, 36 and 38 Muswell Road which had been built in 1885. Eventually Alderman Goulding had a plaque erected in 1949 on No. 40 which is now accepted as the location. It is a pity that Clerkenwell's proposal in 1898 to buy 12 feet of ground for £15 to purchase the well's site was never carried through. No trace of the well is to be seen and Muswell Stream, which it fed, is now culverted, though its course has been traced by experts such as David Harrison.

One of the late Victorian houses at the top of Muswell Road has the name Park View, as it once looked over Wellfield estate to Alexandra Park. Once Edmondson began to build this view was lost. One of his houses on the corner of his Wellfield Avenue with Muswell Road is date-stoned 1901. Wellfield house itself stood approximately where the sorting office is, behind the post office in the Broadway. These postal offices were built by Edmondson (although the street façade was modernised in 1936). Royal Parade extends from the Post Office almost to Muswell Road where the corner is turned by the elegant baroque-styled Palace Mansions building, all erected by Edmondson. Wellfield and Elms Avenue on this estate contain some of Edmondson's most admired properties.

Further south, on the Elms estate, Edmondson replaced the mansion with two curving rows of shopping parades called The Exchange, divided by Dukes Avenue which ran over the grounds. Interestingly Dr Draper noticed in an old view of Bath House, (near this site), that there was a notice saying coaches would depart from The Exchange, and speculated whether Edmondson had used an earlier name. One of the first shop tenants in the Exchange was Sainsbury, then noted for its well-designed, tiled shop interiors and for retailing which did not depend upon the unhygienic outdoor display of foods. The shop transferred to supermarket premises newly built in Fortis Green Road in 1966. Many still remember shopping at the earlier Sainsbury where cheese was cut by a wire and weighed, goods put into paper bags, with customers grouping around the counters and a wooden chair available for those needing to sit.

The estate which Edmondson laid out here was initially called The Station Estate (it was close to Muswell Hill station) and the principal road Station Avenue, perhaps to attract commuters. But Dukes Avenue was soon substituted, matching his prestigious Queens and Princes Avenues. Between No. 26 and No. 28 Dukes Avenue he made a pathway to enable residents to reach the station more quickly. Nearby are some of his most capacious and attractive houses.

Edmondson took advantage of the railway to help build. Cummins reported:

'When building operations were in full swing, and his builders were using between 250,000 and 300,000 bricks a day, Mr Edmondson was obliged to negotiate with the railway company with a view to providing his own siding at the nearest point to Dukes-avenue. The siding was made where the footpath now leads to the station platform and Mr Edmondson had his own engine, which was used to pull the railway trucks arriving

daily with the materials. This novel enterprise was favourably commented upon by the railway magazine as probably the first time that such a thing had been done by a suburban builder, and quite an American method of overcoming a difficult problem.'

When Edmondson completed building on the east side of Colney Hatch Lane he continued on the west side by acquiring North Lodge which he began to build up between 1906 and 1910. Along the Lane he built a row of houses called Sunnyside and behind it Woodberry Crescent.

Edmondson's ideas for his middle class suburb were not confined to shops, flats and houses. He also had other needs of future residents in mind and as a nonconformist he helped several churches get established in the suburb. He gave the site for the Congregational church (now United Reformed) on the corner of Queens Avenue and Tetherdown and sold the site for the Presbyterian church in present day Broadway for half its actual cost. He gave land for a Baptist church in Dukes Avenue whose foundation stone was laid by his wife Isabelle, who was a Baptist, though he was a Congregationalist. (He did not build the church.)

Also in Dukes Avenue was land opposite the Baptist church which he gave as a site for a public library. But as this was not taken up by 1910 it reverted to him. In Queens Avenue he gave the site for a fire station which was built there; since 1931 this site has been occupied by Muswell Hill Library. One of his talents was in music; he was an accomplished pianist, and in Fortis Green Road, next to St James's Parade he built a community centre called the Athenaeum with two concert halls. This was much used by the community till taken over in 1966 for the site of the Sainsbury supermarket, with flats above.

Edmondson also gave liberally to Hornsey Central Hospital, in nearby Park Road, Crouch End, of which he was a trustee and governor, and to the Royal Northern Hospital. He attended Highbury Quadrant congregational church.

In this way Edmondson built the core of the new suburb of Muswell Hill from the acquisition of the first land in 1896 till North Lodge in 1906. Collins and other builders extended the suburb outwards; they included Brondson, Pappin, Rich, Gill, Finnane and Woolnough. But it was Collins who built closest to the centre of Muswell Hill with his Fortismere estate and whose firm was to create the Rookfield estate in a more advanced architectural and town planning style.

William Jefferies Collins (1856-1939) was a bookbinder's son who married a music teacher and had a family of four sons and two daughters: Ralph, Martyn, Herbert, William, Ada and Ethel. Ralph was to become a building contractor, largely working in Southampton. Martyn was killed in the First World War whilst Herbert and William were to take on their father's building work in Muswell Hill after Collins senior too went to Southampton, in 1911. Herbert went to Southampton as well leaving William ('Billy') at Muswell Hill. Collins was a Baptist and one of his undertakings was the rebuilding of Ferme Park church. He built elsewhere in Crouch End, and in 1897 had plans approved by Hornsey UDC for 28 dwelling houses in Church Crescent, built over part of Upton Farm. His firm operated then from Avenue Road, Highgate.

Collins purchased the Fortismere and Firs estates in about 1896 and moved into Fortismere. Samuel Somes JP, who was still living in Fortismere in 1891, must have been one of the first to know that Renton's property was being sold to a builder and that Muswell Hill would change. Although the Somes family had saved The Limes from building in 1865 they did not do the same in 1896. He and the occupant of The Firs moved out.

Detailed plans for building over his new property had been prepared by Collins in 1898 but had to be amended and were not approved by the council till July 1899. Again agreement had to be reached over the width of roads. By December 1899 the council had approved plans for 32 dwelling houses in Grand Avenue. The choice of this name for his main residential road is interesting as in (Sir) Ebenezer Howard's 1898 book about laying out garden cities the main thoroughfare in a diagram is named Grand Avenue; his son Herbert Collins worked at Letchworth, the first garden city planned in accordance with Ebenezer Howard's ideas and might have passed this name on.

In 1901 the council approved a further 152 houses, including 48 in Leaside Avenue, 45 in Fortismere Avenue and 24 in Firs Avenue. By 1902 roads were being made. Collins did not try to emulate Edmondson by building shopping parades on his estate frontages, erecting only Firs Parade opposite Edmondson's St James's Parade, and a small row of shops in Fortis Green. On his undeveloped perimeter sites blocks of apartments were to be erected instead, especially by his son William.

About this time Collins had an unhappy experience about naming one of his roads, falling into dispute with the council, leading to a court case. This was in May 1901 in the Kings Bench Division (Collins v. Hornsey UDC) when Collins appealed against a decision of justices sitting at Highgate about defacing the name of 'a certain street', to wit Collingwood Avenue, contrary to the provisions of section 64 of the Towns Improvement Clauses Act 1847. This Act provided that:

(the UDC) 'shall from time to time cause the houses and buildings in all or any of the streets to be marked with numbers as they think fit and shall cause to put up or be painted on a conspicuous part of some house, building or place near each end, corner or entrance of every such street, the name by which such street is to be known and every person who destroys or pulls down or defaces any such number or name different from the number or name put up shall be liable to a penalty not exceeding forty shillings for every offence'.

The *Hornsey Journal* gave the appeal court report of Collins's transgression:

'The appellant in the year 1899 was the owner of the Fortismere estate and early in the same year submitted to Hornsey Urban District Council plans showing positions and names of certain proposed new streets on the Fortismere estate which he proposed to lay out and construct. One of the streets was named Midhurst Avenue. Ten of the houses were completed and 26 in course of erection. The name was put in the street near one end of it by means of a noticeboard fixed to a post.

Hornsey UDC proposed to substitute Collingwood Avenue. The reason was a Mr William Arnold who lived in a house called Midhurst adjoining the Fortismere estate objected to the name Midhurst being given to the said street. It was renamed Collingwood *but Collins objected. On November 27th 1900 respondents affixed a board with the name Collingwood Avenue thereupon to a house at the end of the said street of which the appellant was the owner. On the same day appellant caused the name of Collingwood Avenue on the board to be obliterated by being painted out. The magistrates were of the opinion the respondents Hornsey UDC had the power under Section 64 of the Act to determine the name.'*

Collins's appeal was dismissed, the Lord Chief Justice remarking that it was not open to the appellant to deface the name of the street. The first duty of putting up the name of the street rested on the local authority.

'Midhurst', the house of William Arnold who had objected to the avenue now called Collingwood being called Midhurst, was just to the west of the Fortismere estate. Arnold did not live there much longer for by 1903 his estate was being developed in its turn, with Midhurst Avenue laid out parallel to Collingwood Avenue. House building seems to have been carried out by different builders over a decade or more, unlike the Edmondson and Collins developments. Where Midhurst Avenue joined Fortis Green some roadside land was left, allowing a welcome green space to be created. Midhurst was demolished when the avenue was laid out but was to be given a replacement in 1921, built at the southern end. Those seeking more details of how Collins built up his Fortismere Estate will find them in Jack Whitehead's *The Growth of Muswell Hill* where dates of building of different sections between 1901 and 1908 are given and house plans provided.

Collins's next major development was the Avenue House estate. Of the three houses there he chose to live in Rookfield rather than Avenue House or Lalla Rookh, probably because this fitted in better with living in one house and building around it, as he had done at Fortismere. The name Rookfield probably derives from the large rookery on Muswell Hill in the nineteenth century, commented upon by Mr Cable, who had been coachman to Mr Herbert Smith of North Lodge, Colney Hatch Lane. *'When the birds started building in March one could hardly hear oneself speak for the tremendous chatter and cawing'*, Mr Cable remembered. Only crows now are to be seen in this area, the rooks presumably having moved out to the countryside once the countryside had left Muswell Hill!

Rookfield was occupied in the 1880s by Mr Collinson of Messrs Collinson and Lock of Oxford Street, according to the reminiscences of Mr H Nobbs, a one time Hornsey rate collector. A manufacturer of artistic furniture the firm amalgamated in 1898 with Messrs. Gillows, an even better known name in this field. Next occupant was Mr A W Gamage, of the well-known but now sadly lost Holborn firm. He must have still been living there in October 1901 for he wrote then to the *Hornsey Journal* complaining about the pond at Lalla Rookh emitting a stench. Collins probably continued to live at Fortismere until 1902 before moving into Rookfield. Avenue House estate had been put up for sale unsuccessfully in 1885 and again in 1891, in each case the auction sale bill describing it as comprising about 23 acres with three fine old residences, with entrance lodges and out-offices, plus Antigua Cottage and Vale Cottage. Collins seems to have made his purchase in 1899. Although Avenue House and Lalla Rookh were

26. William Jefferies Collins built substantial Edwardian houses along Grand Avenue, the principal road on his Fortismere estate.

27. Properties in more advanced architectural style were built by W J Collins's sons on the Rookfield Garden Estate.

demolished to allow building, Rookfield House was still standing in 1912 when Prickett and Ellis advertised it for sale with five acres, 'ripe for development'. This was when William Jefferies Collins had moved to Southampton, leaving the development of what was to be called the Rookfield Garden Estate to his sons. Rookfield house however did not survive; its location was where No. 16 Cranmore Way now stands; Avenue House where Nos 19 and 21 Rookfield Avenue were built; Lalla Rookh's site is now the rear gardens of Nos 23, 25 and 27 Cranmore Way.

Collins began by building houses around the perimeter of the Avenue House estate in St James's Lane and on Muswell Hill. He laid out Etheldene Avenue on the flatter southern end of the site, building in similar style to his Fortismere estate. The new road made a triangle with the Hill and the eastern end of St James's Lane with the infill to become the new Rookfield estate. W J Collins sketched out the initial plan for this which was broadly kept to, as described by Anne Trevett in *Hornsey Historical Society Bulletin 29* (1988) who had been able to discuss the estate with Billy Collins before he died in 1977. But as his sons took over the design of the houses and estate layout they began to apply garden city ideas, utilising architectural concepts developed by Voysey, Baillie Scott, Luytens and other architects who, with town planners Parker and Unwin all worked not more than a few miles sway at Hampstead Garden Suburb, begun in 1907. In consequence the estate is characterised by vernacular inspired architecture in brick; communal space; irregular groupings of houses; much lower densities; and private, gated roads unadopted by the council. (The estate's external appearance has been safeguarded since the 1980s by an Article Four town planning regulation.)

Herbert Collins had had architectural training but William was said to have the greater flair, being a painter who had exhibited at the Royal Academy. Both brothers designed houses for the estate but when in 1913 Rookfield Garden Village Ltd was established it was William Brannan Collins (1883-1877) who was sole director and responsible for development. As already noted, Herbert was to move to Southampton where his father had gone in 1911 and where his brother Ralph was building. He was to be responsible for many Southampton estates as described by Robert Williams in his book *Herbert Collins 1885-1975: Architect and Worker for Peace*. Billy Collins was to contribute many well-designed houses and flats here and in Muswell Hill and a memorial plaque to him was installed on the Rookfield Estate by residents.

Edmondson had created a middle class suburb in place of the rural village and Collins had added substantially to its residential avenues. But these were not the only builders. Where estates were obtainable other builders began to work. Not acquired in the centre of Muswell Hill by Edmondson, for example, were Summerlands and Belle Vue at the crest of the hill. Summerlands was taken by builder Thomas Finnane. His plans to lay out Summerlands Gardens and an adjacent parade, overlooking the present day roundabout, were approved by the council in 1904. The mansion building is distinguished by a circular set of wood railings on the roof once known locally as Maiden's Walk. They were restored in 1998 but the small green dome which originally topped them was not reinstated. Finnane was to have a vital role in the shaping of Muswell Hill by helping to create the roundabout, as I shall show in the next chapter. Belle Vue, where Frederic Harrison had once lived, was acquired by the Express Dairy and a large milk depot created. On the street frontage they built a

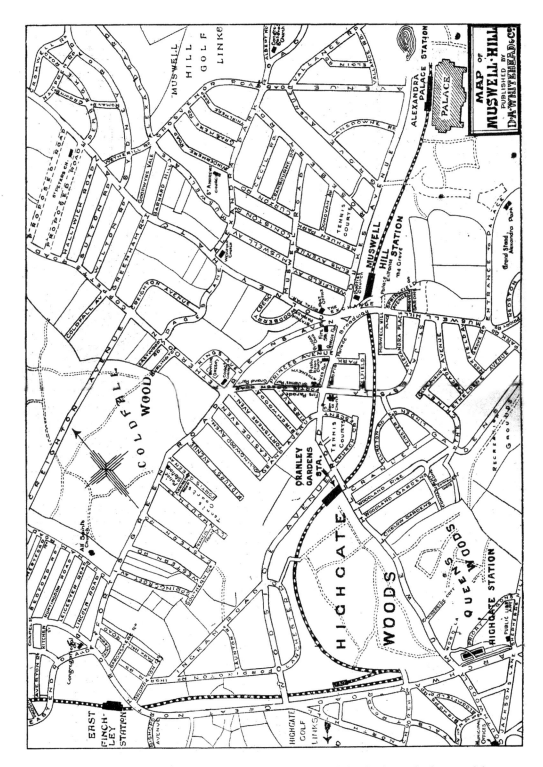

28. This street plan, included in a locally published 1914 guidebook, shows the layout of the new
suburb, by then firmly established.

refreshment room, set back, a building distinguished by the date 1900 in Art Nouveau style. This has long been converted into a wine bar but the building has happy memories for me as a place where Teresa and I could take tea whilst shopping. (In our youth we had the Express, Lyons and ABC tea rooms to choose from and McDonald's was unheard of; Muswell Hill's 'Joe Lyons' was at 51 The Broadway, now a fruiterer's, its coloured glass windows still there.)

The side of Muswell Hill Broadway between Finnane's Summerlands Gardens and Edmondson's Hillfield development escaped major change probably because it was in fragmented ownership. It contained a line of Victorian domestic properties such as Hillfield Cottages, Stanley villa and Rosemount, mostly lost by some interwar rebuilding, such as for Lloyd's bank, leaving a legacy uncharacteristic of Muswell Hill's homogeneity of style. The remnants of a pair of Gothic style villas remain. Behind these properties Muswell Hill was to contain an entertainment centre, as I shall also describe later.

The major extension of the new suburb was to the north east where ground belonging to the owners of Alexandra Palace and Park estate became ripe for building at long last. Development on this estate land had begun in the 1880s, as mentioned earlier, on the Clerkenwell Detached area. The undeveloped east side of Colney Hatch Lane began to acquire houses, though when No. 40, a doctor's house was built in 1888 only two other villas were there; by 1903 they had been joined by ten others, as well as a Methodist church. At the 1899 enquiry (see p.59) Hornsey's chief engineer, Mr Edwin Lovegrove, reported that of its 64.5 acres about 50 were laid out for building. Of the 209 houses erected some 161 were occupied, giving a population of 1,100. Edmondson's development and a unified local authority control after Clerkenwell Detached was absorbed by Hornsey, now speeded up work.

Between 1889 and 1894 a new road across Clerkenwell Detached called Alexandra Park Road had been marked out connecting Colney Hatch Lane with the overland railway station at Wood Green (now called Alexandra Palace). Its first part followed the line of a former path to Tottenham Wood farmhouse but it then ran parallel with the northern boundary of the park. In 1900 an Act of Parliament transferred ownership of the park and Alexandra Palace to a group of local authorities who made the purchase because they feared that the park would be built over and local people deprived of open space. The remaining palace company land north of the palace now had new commercial potential because of the urbanisation of Muswell Hill and was soon to be covered with residential avenues in the Edwardian era, including a northern portion of the park (though the lake area was saved).

One large scale builder here was Charles Rook who erected 10 shops on Alexandra Park Road and 365 houses in Coniston, Curzon, Cecil, Cranbourne Roads and in Muswell and Donovan Avenues and in Methuen Park. He built both sides along the whole length of Rosbery Road. His own house at 33 Cecil Road, a double fronted, three-storey building, was ornately decorated with a large, carved head of himself under the porch. In a frieze under the second floor window he showed his wife's hand with a chain bracelet clasped into his own hand. Charles Rook died in a building accident. His shops with their 1907 date stone, extended in the 1930s, remain a valued asset. Another builder in this area was Josiah Brondson who, for example, built on the south side of Cranbourne Road whilst Rook built on the north side (both builders used architects).

29. Builder Charles Rook's magnificently decorated house in Cecil Road; it bears a 1903 date stone.

30. Auguste Jaeger, 'Nimrod' of the Enigma Variations, photographed in 1905 outside 37 Curzon Road where he lived from 1902 till his death in 1909. Visited here by Elgar he is seen with Professor Sanford (left) and Countess Olga Wood (in carriage) and with his own children.

The land on the north side of Alexandra Park Road had been acquired in 1893 from the palace company by the newly formed Muswell Hill Golf Club and a course laid out, extended to eighteen holes in 1895. They gave up this land in 1899 and laid out new links on their present site (later expanded) to the east. When in 1906 Wood Green council bought Tottenham Wood farmhouse to build a school near it they leased the house to the golfers as a clubhouse. (When Rhodes Avenue school was built here in 1930 replacing a temporary school the golfers moved out and the farmhouse was demolished leaving only its portico). The rest of the former golf links were built over, the avenues being given the names of English lakes: Windermere, Grasmere and Thirlmére. The former Middleton Road opposite was also renamed after a lake, Coniston, probably to save postal confusion with roads in Bowes Park, Wood Green and Hornsey all also named after Sir Hugh Myddleton of the New River.

Also on the north side of Alexandra Park Road a site was bought by the Church of England and a temporary iron church put up before St Andrew's was built, designed by the architect of St James's, Muswell Hill. This was J S Alder (1847-1919) who lived at 'Hillside' in Muswell Road and who was to become a sidesman at the church, the foundation stone for which was laid in 1903. It survives in truncated form following restoration after bomb damage in the war.

By the work of these builders a whole new residential estate called Alexandra Park was thus added to the core of Muswell Hill; similar building styles were used thus making for an architectural unity. For by the time Muswell Hill and district came to be built the familiar Victorian terraced house styles (to be seen for example in Stroud Green which was built up in the 1870s) had given way to new architectural fashions.

These derived from the so-called 'Queen Anne' style pioneered from 1860 by architects Norman Shaw and W Eden Nesfield and which owed something to the plainer seventeenth century English brick houses designed under Dutch influence. This became associated with the Arts and Crafts movement which sought a return to traditional handicrafts (a gesture against industrialisation) and to traditional vernacular building styles, methods and materials. There emerged an Arts and Crafts Free Style which mixed classical forms such as Baroque with vernacular detailing, freeing the domestic house from the ponderousness of the Victorian builder and improving its aesthetic appearance. Builders were using this freer style by the time Muswell Hill came to be built. The new 'avenues' which surrounded the new shopping parades (nothing so common as a Victorian 'road' or a working class 'street') were filled with substantial terraced houses in brick with stone dressings, to which were added ornate pargetting work in plaster and features in white painted wood.

One of the pleasures of living in Muswell Hill is to walk the avenues such as Dukes, Wellfield or Elms, noticing the way street corners are turned, often with turrets, the decoration responding to the mass and shape of the building; then the wonderful pargetting, the bay windows, porches, little balconies, and small-paned upper windows which make the house exteriors such a delight. These features give Muswell Hill its architectural character and draw people to live in it. The large, roomy houses also have attractive interior features.

31. Edwardian domestic architecture seen at its best in Dukes Avenue.

32. Kings Avenue at its junction with Queens Avenue.

Fortis Green also sees 'Arts and Crafts' fully expressed in Fairport House at the eastern end with next to it The Gables, mansions with art nouveau railings at third floor level. Birchwood Mansions in Fortis Green Road, between Birchwood and Firs Avenues, is a favourite with many, built in a style similar to a Hampstead Garden City gatehouse, so reducing the impact of its bulk. A stable courtyard for horses (complete with tethering ring) has survived behind it although adapted to other purposes. Billy Collins (who built all these properties) stabled his own coach and horses here.

All these new residential avenues were laid out between the old roads. Most were terraced and without garages for this was still the age of horse transport. Here and there a surviving detached coach house may be seen, as for example near the corner of Rosebery and Alexandra Park Roads. Traffic was not too heavy, so that pedestrians were able to wander across roads, as the old Edwardian postcard views show, something we envy today. A new road was constructed which connected the new suburb with the old Great North Road at East Finchley. This was Creighton Avenue which in 1900 was cut through ancient Coldfall Wood. Early views show the road lined each side with woodland. Imposing properties began to be built along it, westwards from where it started in Pages Lane. The new road was named after the then Bishop of London, Dr Mandell Creighton (1843-1901), the woods having been part of the Bishop's ancient manorial holdings (there had been no defined parish boundary between Hornsey and Finchley here until the Enclosure Acts, the land having been used as the bishop's park). Dr Mandell Creighton was a noted English historian who became the first professor of ecclesiastical history at Cambridge in 1894 before being made bishop of Peterborough and then in 1897 bishop of London. In June 1900, the year before he died, he laid the foundation stone of the rebuilt St James's church.

A little to the south, the east side of Tetherdown was completed in this period, with Kings Avenue connecting it with the new Queens Avenue, houses being built in Tetherdown and Kings Avenue by J Pappin of Stoke Newington. This land seems from the 1865 map to have been once the grounds of Fortis Cottage, a substantial building later reputed to be derelict. The estate was purchased by James Hall Renton in 1876 to add to his contiguous Fortis House property. T Woolnough of 17 Bryanstone Road, Crouch End was another builder who put up houses in Kings Avenue. His firm had been responsible for another Muswell Hill estate development, that of Delaporte on the north west corner of St James's Lane and Muswell Hill. His plans for this development were approved by the council in September 1898, subject to widening of both roads by ten feet or more. Proposals were for thirteen houses on Muswell Hill, seven in St James's Lane and ten in Alexandra Place. Woolnough also built in Dukes Avenue, Palace Gardens and Grove Avenue.

In this way other builders aided Edmondson's grand project of a new suburb. What transport and other services were to be provided for it? How was it to develop as a community?

Chapter 6

Servicing the Suburb

Muswell Hill became primarily a residential suburb for householders working in central London, though some of the population were engaged in providing local services. There was however no industry of any significance and no large group of manual workers. Muswell Hill was a 'respectable' place with five churches and the sedate behaviour approved at the time. Interestingly it has been argued that a factor determining its attractiveness and status was its position on high ground; this is said to be also true for Highgate, Hampstead, Crystal Palace, Harrow and other places in the London hinterland which are also frequently adjacent to poorer areas.

Its geographical attractiveness was aided by the survival of the woods on its southern side. Modern aerial photographs confirm that these make a formidable barrier (of about 120 acres) impeding building, providing Muswell Hill with a kind of southern frontier. The public acquisition of Alexandra Park in 1900 also ensured a green belt on its north east side, to which can be added on the north side the surviving fragments of Coldfall Wood and not far off to the south the green acres of Crouch End Playing Fields which abut Queens Wood.

The arrival of middle class residents in Muswell Hill was part of London's outward expansion, as Stephen Inwood maintains in his *History of London* (Macmillan 1998). The middle class, growing fast, although unable to afford a second home in the country were yet able to pay a daily bus or train fare to their offices, argues Inwood. The movement outwards was aided by rising real wages, shorter working hours and lower transport costs. Inwood believes that transport improvements were an important liberating factor, that is: stage coaches from the 1820s, omnibuses from the 1830s, trains from the 1850s, horse trams from the 1870s, and after 1900 motor buses, electric trams and deep level tubes. The mixture of town and country in the suburbs was appealing, especially for former country dwellers; it also allowed the development of domestic private life, which meant respect for privacy, 'respectability', and social segregation and also the domestication and isolation of women based on separation of work and home.

The fact that Muswell Hill was still seen as countryside is illustrated by the case of Charles Landstone (1890-1978), a playwright and theatre manger of Viennese origin who was to become an Arts Council drama director. In his autobiography *I Gate-Crashed* (1976) he explains that his family moved to Muswell Hill when he was sixteen because his elder sister had developed tuberculosis and it was thought that the near-country would be good for her health in between stays in a sanatorium (though sadly she was to die within eight years).

> *'In the year 1907', he wrote, 'we moved from Kilburn to the comparatively new suburb of Muswell Hill which was largely undeveloped and had only a few main roads running through the fields. We lived in Cranley Gardens which was a made up road over a mile in length but with only one row of houses, semi-detached villas at its northern end, numbering 1 – 45. We were in no. 35 and south of us for nearly half a mile on our side of the road were a series of tennis courts which were the Mecca of all the enthusiasts in north London. They arrived in droves on Saturdays at the railway station at the top of our road. When we moved to Muswell Hill only the wealthiest classes bought the houses they lived in. We paid an annual rent of about £40 in Cranley Gardens'.*

The railway station, named Cranley Gardens, had opened in 1902 on the branch line to Alexandra Palace. Positioned in Muswell Hill Road next to Woodside Avenue it served the new avenues on the southern side. These included Woodland Rise and Woodland Gardens, laid out over the former 11-acre Woodlands estate where the Lehmanns had entertained. These new roads, built by R Metherall, lay between Cranley Gardens and the earlier Onslow Gardens.

This branch railway with stations at Highgate, Cranley Gardens, Muswell Hill and Alexandra Palace, played an important part in the early development of the suburb, allowing residents to travel to London. Used effectively by Edmondson to transport building materials it was now given a new lease of life. By 1910 there were to be 61 trains each way daily, running either to Kings Cross, Moorgate via Farringdon, or to Broad Street. The first train did not depart until 7.14 am, unlike other districts where very early morning trains ran for workmen. The journey to Kings Cross was scheduled to take about 20 minutes. From 1897 Mr A Craddock of the Green Man provided a landau, a cab and a trap for hire from outside Muswell Hill station. The old ale house had by then already been given a brick-built hotel extension on its southern side designed in 1884 by J Goldsworthy. Perhaps this was intended for Alexandra Park visitors, though in the 1890s the park and palace were mostly closed, due to financial problems.

London's motive power in the late nineteenth century was still the horse, with nearly a quarter of a million pulling road vehicles of all kinds in 1900. Of these some 80,000 pulled omnibuses and trams and this kind of transport arrived at Muswell Hill in the form of horse buses (but not horse trams) making an impact which helped to shape the new suburb's centre. In April 1901 twelve horse buses commenced running between Charing Cross and Muswell Hill; each was drawn by three horses and made five journeys a day. Services to other destinations made 24 journeys a day.

The consequence was a need for a 'stand' or stopping place between these journeys and this meant a problem for the builder, Thomas Finnane. He solved it by writing a successful letter to the council in June 1902:

> 'I understand that it is the intention to have a bus stand paved close to the footpath, and immediately opposite the shops and flats I am about to erect. May I be permitted to point out that a bus stand in that position will be very objectionable from many points of view? And considering the amount of land I am giving up for street improvement purposes I think it is only fair to have the buses moved to, say, the centre of the street. Although wishing to be reasonable as possible in every way, on behalf of my tenants and myself I must respectfully protest against this proposal'.

Finnane had agreed on gaining approval for the laying out of the 'Summerlands Estate' to give up land for the public highway 386 feet in length and varying from 16 feet to one foot in width, an area of about 310 yards. (Motorists driving up Muswell Hill and into the Broadway by the roundabout pass over the land Finnane gave to the council). This gift must have carried some weight for the upshot was that:

> 'The committee recommended that the paved stand for the omnibuses should be placed at the top of Muswell-hill, next to the Plantation, in the middle of the roadway, if the consent of the police authorities was obtained. The cost of the stand would be about £200 increasing the estimated cost of the improvement by that amount. The committee accordingly further recommend that application should be made to the Local Government Board for their sanction to the borrowing of £680'.

By mid-August 1902 the stand for omnibuses at Muswell Hill was completed, providing a paved area measuring 100 feet by 12 feet. It was in this way that one of the main features of Muswell Hill, the roundabout in which buses are parked, came about. For horse buses were followed by petrol buses (from 1912) and subsequently by diesel buses and the stand grew larger and absorbed the old Plantation. All because Mr Finnane wrote a letter to the council. (Metal railings existed round the Plantation in the nineteenth century but were replaced by a ring of smart tall railings on urbanisation; the area encircled has gradually increased.)

The bus stand at the road junction spawned other features. In February 1903, for example, a clock was fixed over Sainsbury's shop in The Exchange. It is a pity that this asset, to be seen in old postcard views, disappeared in later years. (The shops opened late in 1902 in The Exchange, though in November 1902 drains were still being laid there, giving rise to complaints that the existing pavement was barricaded and the public forced to walk in a dirty road between omnibus horses for several yards).

The clock would have been useful for bus drivers to keep to schedules but the omnibus company did not seem to go out of its way to provide any other kind of convenience. First came a shelter which owed its existence to the humanitarian feelings of local residents and the collection of donations to pay for it. Opened in April 1904 it was described in *The Morning Leader*:

> 'London's First Busmen's Shelter.....the neat tiled structure cost just £80.....the Gas Company have connected the shelter with the main free of cost....Mr Samual Cook of North Bank, Pages-lane, who gave largely to the funds of the shelter, opened the building'.

33. Horse buses are to be seen (right) outside the Exchange parade of shops; the roundabout was formerly known as the Plantation.

34. Petrol buses have replaced horse buses, and a shelter for busmen provided in the roundabout (left).

But all needs have to be catered for and in 1907 the council Works Committee

'recommended the construction of an underground convenience, for men only, on the north side of the planted enclosure at the top of Muswell Hill, the estimated cost comprising seven stalls being £450'.

The proposal was adopted after long discussion. Facilities for ladies do not seem to have been supplied till 1925. (It was then that excavating workmen found signs of the old village pond).

The first bus provider was a local man. Mr Henry Pope was described as the Muswell Hill omnibus pioneer when he died, aged 76, in August 1919. His obituary said that Mr Pope had been:

'a large brake proprietor at premises near Archway Tavern and was the pioneer of an omnibus service to Muswell Hill, a one-horse bus with accommodation for 12 people inside. Fares had to be paid to the driver, there being no conductor.....These buses ran from The Exchange, Muswell Hill to the Woodman and were a great acquisition to the neighbourhood at the time....Subsequently Mr Pope supplanted this service with the first three-horse bus that plied between Muswell Hill and the Archway Tavern'.

The road surfaces were not then macadam but gravelled earth, dusty in summer, muddy in winter and, as Finnane implied, horse droppings often made them 'very objectionable'. The *Hornsey Journal* commented in 1903:

'to walk from the foot to the summit of Colney Hatch Lane this weather is to pass over something which resembles the slough of despond by Bunyan'.

To overcome the problem stone setts connected one pavement to the next to give a dryer surface; good examples are to be seen where Firs Avenue enters Fortis Green Road or at Woodberry Crescent, parallel to Colney Hatch Lane.

If you were lucky when you got home there would be a cross-bar set in the wall by your front door with which you could scrape mud from your shoes. In this period too 'spats' were worn by men, cloth coverings buttoned over the tops of your footwear to protect them and your ankles; this is a boyhood memory for me as is a fashion (or a need) long passed, the buttoned, knee-length 'gaiters' I once had to wear.

Maintenance of roads was a responsibility of the local council which grew more powerful in 1903 when Hornsey became a Borough instead of an Urban District. In that year a council sub-depot to help with highway work was established for Muswell Hill. This was in Fortis Green, behind St James's school, and was bought from the Ecclesiastical Commissioners for £5,210. On the site were stabling for seven horses, sheds for stores, a men's mess room and other facilities. It was sold off by the council in the early 1990s and has been replaced by housing, with a new entrance road from Tetherdown called Spring Gardens. Part of this housing site had been occupied by garages and the passageway over which Spring Gardens was built had contained for many years a neglected early form of petrol pump.

It was not until 1910 that the nation's roads began to be given a hard crust in the form of tarmac, an Edwardian invention. The cost of road work came from the annual road licence and the tax on petrol which the government introduced in 1909.

In 1914 Hornsey Borough pioneered the manufacture of asphalt from clinker residue at the refuse destructor and used it satisfactorily for surfacing many miles of local roads. Most of the artificial stone paving slabs used in the footways were also manufactured at the destructor, as well as the characteristic purple stone materials used in front garden walls.

Trees were planted by the council as Hornsey became urbanised. The rule was that they were not planted in roads less than 45 feet wide and according to one councillor this had induced freeholders laying out estates to provide wider roads than the minimum of 40 feet stipulated by the by-laws. Muswell Hill was to have trees planted along most of its prestigious new avenues.

Street lighting was by gas, a service begun in 1869 by the Hornsey Gas Company, though with only a sparse number of lights in rural days. Electric lighting began to be introduced after the council had bought out the North Metropolitan Electricity Supply company in 1903 and built a generating station near Hornsey railway station, though the introduction of electric lighting throughout the borough seems to have been slow. Lighting and better road services would have been welcomed by the increasing number of cyclists. From the 1880s the standard bicycle, invented then, had been an important improvement in personal transport, said to have played a vital role in giving new freedoms, especially to women.

Road vehicles in the first years of the new suburb remained largely horse-drawn. A few rich men such as Edmondson would have invested in one of the new 'horseless carriages' but numbers were few. ('Scores of times (Edmondson) made his chauffeur stop the car and give me a lift to Muswell Hill' William Cummins wrote, providing an example of a rich man who did not necessarily drive himself; early motorist Rudyard Kipling is another).

Despite their early appearance on Britain's roads I doubt whether it was foreseen that this new form of transport would expand into universal use and multiply so much over the decades. Car ownership on a large scale did not really develop until the 1960s, even though before 1939 car use was widespread and the motor lorry was replacing the horse and cart. My father born in 1888 never drove. I did not take driving lessons until I was about 40 years old. By contrast my son and daughter both passed their driving test, first attempt, at the minimum legal age of 17. Such is a typical effect it has had on different generations.

Muswell Hill's built environment was largely established before the age of the motor car. Most of Edmondson's and Collins's terraces are without garages; not until the 1920s did the fashion for semi-detached houses with garages find mass expression in the outer suburbs. Older detached properties often had a coach house which could serve as a garage, and stabling generally was converted into motor car storage and servicing. When Billy Collins built Birchwood Mansions in 1907 he erected elegant stabling at the rear and this was used later for cars.

It was in 1907 that W Collins submitted plans for a 'motor shed' in Firs Avenue but these were not approved. When were the first motor garages so named? The *Oxford English Dictionary* cites 1902 as the first recorded usage, so by using the term 'motor shed' Collins might have been a little behind the times. One of the more interesting properties in Muswell Hill can be found by walking down the side of Tetherdown Hall to the rear of Woodside flats, built in the early 1920s. Here is a group of brick-built garages, the design obviously modelled on the blocks of stables you see when you visit some country house, complete with a little tower feature. Are these Muswell Hill's first block of purpose-built garages?

The consequence of Muswell Hill being built just before the age of the internal combustion engine is of course everywhere to be seen, with parked cars narrowing nearly every road and spoiling some of the original elegance of the streets. Indeed the arrival of kerb-side metal boxes in great numbers, particularly in the 1990s, has perhaps done more than anything else to change Muswell Hill's appearance especially if you add to that all the other associated developments from white and yellow lines to traffic islands, pedestrian crossings and traffic lights.

Horse transport for the delivery of goods continued however for many decades. Behind Edmondson's parades are to be found service roads, nearly all cul-de-sacs, along which horse-drawn carts could bring supplies to the individual shops. Avenue Mews, between Princes and Queens Avenues, is lined on the north side by mews buildings where carts and horses were stabled. Before the war horse delivery was a common feature and it persisted in use by milk distributors and coal merchants into the 1960s. A few brewery drays can occasionally still be seen, though the shire horses that draw them are used mainly for their publicity value.

Other replacements for the horse began to appear by the start of the twentieth century. The electric tram, for example, which replaced horse-drawn trams, extended their routes far out into the suburbs. Although no electric (or horse-drawn) tram reached the centre of Muswell Hill a tram service from Turnpike Lane along Priory Road began in 1907, terminating either at the foot of Muswell Hill or proceeding to Alexandra Palace, (there using single-deck vehicles). Passengers alighting in the Park could reach Dukes Avenue by a new pathway under the railway bridge. Electric trams also ran along Archway Road after the archway was replaced by a wider bridge in 1900.

At that time quite a stir was caused in Muswell Hill when the Middlesex County Council considered applying for an order from the Light Tramways Commissioners to construct a branch line from Archway Road, along Muswell Hill Road to the roundabout, and then down Dukes Avenue. It would then go past what is today The Avenue and Vallance Road and proceed along Palace Gates Road, over the Great Northern Railway, onto Wood Green. It was the residents rather than the GNR who seemed to take the lead in opposing it. The arguments that they used against it were various.

Electric traction provided a great element of danger, travelling at up to 12 to 15 miles per hour. The proposed route had extreme gradients and curves. If it was the intention to pave with granite setts, these were greasy after rain and dangerous to horses. Tall trees might short circuit the electric current. The topic disappeared from the local newspaper so it would seem that the lobbyists won. Recent proposals for a bus service along Dukes Avenue have received a similar frosty reception.

Perhaps the petrol bus was more acceptable than the electric tram to the residents of Muswell Hill. With the invention of the internal combustion engine experimental models began to be built, with London's first regular motor bus service beginning on 19th October 1899 between Kennington and Victoria station, the motor attached to a horse-bus chassis. Progress was facilitated by the 1903 Motor Car Act which raised the speed limit for 3-ton vehicles from 1st January 1904, the dates when vehicle number plates first came into use.

The development of the famous B-type omnibus introduced into public service in October 1910 by the London & General Omnibus Company Ltd represented an important step forward. The horse bus by now was in retreat for in October 1910 the number of petrol buses licensed in London equalled for the first time the number of horse buses licensed: 1,142 of each type. By 1912 the petrol bus had taken over on most London routes.

There is a fine photograph of four B-type petrol buses lined up at Muswell Hill roundabout. The double-deckers advertise a play called *The Bear Leaders* which opened at the Comedy Theatre on 1st February 1912, thus dating the photograph approximately. The photo was probably taken to mark the start of petrol bus services to Muswell Hill in place of horse buses. The buses are all No. 4 and are scheduled to run to Victoria station via Archway. A more significant route was the single decker No. 111 service introduced by the London & General Omnibus Company in 1914 which ran via Crouch End Broadway to Finsbury Park, where tube services were available. (Today this still remains in the guise of the W7, an important route to work for many Muswell Hill residents.) For the Great Northern Railway however it spoilt their trade as former train passengers transferred to the new bus and reduced their income. It responded to the challenge by claiming that buses damaged the railway bridges they passed over such as the one by Muswell Hill station. The bus company countered that argument by keeping to single-deck buses but running them more frequently.

Additional services were also demanded by the middle class residents of Muswell Hill, including that other communications improvement, the telephone. In September 1902 the *Hornsey Journal* commented that it was curious that 'in this great town of 70,000 there was no telephone exchange'. It finally arrived on 7th November 1907 when 'Hornsey' opened in Crouch End Broadway. 'Hornsey' was to be the exchange name for the whole area, including Muswell Hill, until 1924 when it was renamed 'Mountview'. (You dialled MOU followed by the number until growing telephone use in post Second World War years led to letters being replaced by numbers such as 340). In 1928 Muswell Hill got its own exchange when TUDor opened in Grand Avenue. Only a limited number of homes had telephones installed in the early years but other users went to telephone call offices installed in shops, at railway stations, and in post offices, a development begun only in 1884, although the telephone system had begun to operate in the late 1870s. Muswell Hill's first public call office opened in the Post Office in Colney Hatch Lane on 12th April 1907.

Pavement telephone boxes were the next logical step and these began to appear in the nation's streets in many designs and different systems; one for example had doors operated by a coin in a slot. By 1911 the General Post Office had taken over the provision of the kiosks from private enterprise and after 1918 it introduced a standard telephone box known as Kiosk No. 1. These pavement installations in precast concrete were at first seen as obstructions. But a new red kiosk designed by Giles

Gilbert Scott arrived in 1926 in London and this evolved into the classic K6 box of 1936, destined to be the design most widely used. In 1999 Muswell Hill had some of these boxes reintroduced after they were swept away in the 1980s. Phone boxes are still wanted, as is evidenced by a 1999 letter to *The Times* which reported that a four year old, pointing to a roadside telephone box said: 'That's where you go if you don't have a mobile'.

The most familiar Post Office legacy is still the red letter-box. The age of these can be roughly determined by the royal cypher. Here I must point out that Rex is the Latin word for King and Regina for Queen. The box outside St James's church bears the letters VR i.e. Victoria Regina (Queen Victoria who reigned 1837-1901) as does the one on the corner of Pages Lane and Colney Hatch Lane. But many post boxes in Muswell Hill have the cypher E VII R i.e. Edward VII Rex (King Edward VII reigned 1901-1910) and form one of the largest groupings of Edwardian letter boxes in the country. Some have been replaced or supplemented by later boxes but mostly these are the ones to be found in Muswell Hill's Edwardian avenues.

The post box played a very important role in the Edwardian era. Before the widespread use of the telephone the post was the method more often used to convey messages speedily, the telegram being reserved for emergencies. The low levels of postal traffic compared with today, the well manned sorting offices, and deliveries past 9pm by hard working postmen meant that an item posted in the morning would usually reach any English destination the same day. Muswell Hill residents would have not been slow to use this quick way of communicating with others.

This was the golden era for the picture postcard, at its heyday between 1895 and 1915. Relaxation of postal regulations, allowing $5\frac{1}{2}$ inch by $3\frac{1}{2}$ inch cards with a picture on one side and a message and address on the other to be sent with a halfpenny stamp saw their use burgeon. In addition street photographers with plate cameras provided good views of the new streets which residents could send to their friends. These Edwardian picture postcards have been a boon to local historians and have become a collector's eldorado, with high prices paid for cards of quality. Today the use of the picture postcard seems confined to holiday travellers.

The provision of national newspapers, which in Edwardian times was the prime means of circulating news, was the particular concern of William R Cummins who first came to Muswell Hill in 1896 as a teenage newsboy selling papers near the Green Man, taking $7\frac{1}{2}$ old pence on his first morning in days when newspapers cost one old halfpenny. He was to become a successful businessman with newsagent and stationery shops at No. 5 The Exchange (the shop still bears his name) and at No. 21 Station Parade. Provision of a local newspaper specifically for Muswell Hill was also his concern and in 1907 he started *The Muswell Hill Record* for which in 1915 he founded a new printing works in Muswell Hill Broadway at premises located to the rear of present day Crocodile Antiques. In due course he owned several retail stationery businesses (letter writing was more common in the days before the telephone became pre-eminent), two retail florist's shops and a nursery of over one acre. Cummins used to go to Fleet Street in the early hours of the morning to collect national newspapers and in 1906 he was able to bring the parliamentary election results to Muswell Hill to a waiting crowd estimated at 4,000 people. He was thanked by the Earl of Ronaldshay for bringing news of Ronaldshay's re-election as Conservative MP for Hornsey.

The first local newspaper was the *Hornsey Hornet* begun 1866, followed by the *North Middlesex Chronicle* of the late 1870s. One of the most popular today is the *Hornsey Journal* which began as the *Seven Sisters and Finsbury Park Journal* in 1879. By the time it moved in 1885 to 33 Crouch Hill it had become the *Hornsey and Finsbury Park Journal and North Islington Standard*. Its premises in the late twentieth century were in Tottenham Lane, Crouch End. In the 1990s it began issuing different editions for different areas, with a separate one for Muswell Hill, a practice adopted by other local newspapers such as the *Hampstead & Highgate Express* which began a *Broadway* edition aimed at Muswell Hill and Crouch End. The *Express* seems have to begun in 1860 possibly in Highgate as the *Weekly Express*, as suggested by John Richardson in his history of Highgate. George Jealous who owned the Hampstead and Highgate Express from 1862 also founded the *Hornsey Journal* in 1879, but sold it in 1884. Changing to Times typeface the *Express* moved news onto its front page in 1939, a practice adopted by the *Hornsey Journal* in 1947.

Advertising was a feature of Victorian and Edwardian ways of life, as photographs show. Not subject to today's planning constraints, advertising hoardings were to be found on many buildings. A postcard view shows one above the shops opposite the post office. The protection of this hoarding saved the nameplate 'Station Parade' from removal when in 1960 this name was supplanted by that of Muswell Hill Broadway. I included this unusual survival in my *A Walk Around Muswell Hill* written in the 1980s but I have since had phone calls saying it cannot be seen. It seems to have disappeared about the time the shops below it were converted to O'Neill's public house. Another advertisement which has survived, though which at the time of writing is disgracefully spoilt by graffiti, is the one painted on the side wall of 114 Muswell Hill Broadway, adjacent to Marks and Spencer. This advertisement on the end of the former Victoria Parade reads 'Army Club cigarettes 20 for 1/- 10 for 6d.' It must have remained there for some six decades, at times also protected by a hoarding over it, though recent efforts to put a new one over it were disallowed by the planning authorities; today a half-sized hoarding now sits below it.

Cummins's printing works and the offices of The *Muswell Hill Record*, at the then postal address of 18 & 19 Broadway, were close to those of Bond & White, builders merchants at no. 16 Broadway, another local firm whose products were to be essential to the development of Muswell Hill. Joan Schwitzer has related the history of this firm in *Hornsey Historical Bulletin 20* (1979) tracing it back to 1879 when Charles White was a local builder and decorator. In 1900 he went into partnership with James Bond (another name with a different meaning today!). Bond left in 1909 for Buckinghamshire but the White family expanded the firm, meeting the needs of building contractors working in the area as builders merchants, providing another kind of service.

35. The advertising hoarding covers up the name plate Station Parade in Colney Hatch Lane, opposite the post office; today such a hoarding would be unlikely to gain planning approval.

36. Pulham's the butchers survived at the fomer 16 Victoria Parade near the junction with St James's Lane (now 26 The Broadway) till the 1980s.

In 1913 H E White rented a one-storey shed next to an old domestic building on Broadway which in 1927 was demolished so that Lloyd's Bank could be built on the corner of Summerland Gardens. Bond and White followed suit and built a brick building on their site which was their sales shop until the 1970s when the lease ran out and the firm was forced to move the sales shop to the Odeon complex in order to remain in the Muswell Hill shopping centre. (Bond & White's Broadway site was taken over by Budgen's supermarket which later gave way to Marks and Spencer). The firm's main depot for materials was their site at Queens Wood, acquired in 1916 and still functioning.

Of those shops established in the early days of Muswell Hill it is interesting to note others that survived. Already mentioned is Martyn's the grocers, who have been in what was no. 12 Queens Parade from the beginning. Another early arrival in this parade at no. 15 was WH Smith & Son, newsagents which still occupy a shop they took in Edwardian times. The corner premises, no.19 Queens Parade seems always to have been wine and spirit merchants, as they are in 1999, but under different firms. Further along, no. 3 Princes Parade was early occupied by Edward W Langton, watchmaker; a jeweller traded under this name here until 1998. Across the road at no. 16 Victoria Parade, near St James's Lane, was another early arrival, Pulham & Sons, butchers, a shop which survived till the 1980s. Carpenter's the ironmongers was also an early arrival, trading in the corner shop, 7 & 8 Victoria Parade until the early 1980s. HSBC, NatWest and Barclays all trade in premises built as banks for their predecessors, though altered. After a battle in the 1990s the post office remains at its Edwardian site. There may be other examples of shops providing services which still remain from the foundation years.

Local authority services to the new suburb were strengthened when in 1903 Hornsey became, instead of an urban district council, a municipal borough, the second in the county of Middlesex to be formed. It tried later to be made into a County Borough (whose responsibilities matched that of a county) but was not successful, despite its increased population. The borough had a mayor and from 1907 thirty councillors and ten aldermen (the office of alderman no longer exists). In 1910 Muswell Hill ward had three councillors, two of whom lived in Dukes Avenue and the third at 14 Queens Avenue, the latter being the mayor, Councillor Alfred Yeatman. Despite strong Liberal (which often meant non-conformist) representation the council was to be dominated by Municipal Reformers, later Conservatives.

The many council responsibilities included municipal housing (the Coldfall estate was to be built at Muswell Hill 1924-26), drainage, highways, street lighting, tree planting, refuse collection, recreational facilities (Coldfall Woods became a responsibility in 1928), education (an elementary school was built at Muswell Hill in 1913 and Coldfall School in 1928) and libraries (not provided till 1931 in Muswell Hill). The borough also collected the rates which in 1902 stood at seven shillings in the pound on the assessed value of each domestic property. In those days account books were all written by hand (my own monthly bank statements were hand written when I first opened an account in 1945).

Health was a particular responsibility and Hornsey's record had been good with comparatively low rates of sickness and death, leading the 1906 borough guide to describe it as 'Healthy Hornsey'. Medical inspection of schoolchildren began in 1905 after the teaching of personal hygiene from 1904. Food hygiene was to be the subject of a borough campaign. Infectious diseases, such as diphtheria and scarlet fever, were tackled and maternity and child welfare services were provided, including dental treatment at welfare centres.

Protection and law enforcement were the responsibility of the Metropolitan Police force from 1840, with a station in Hornsey manned by four police sergeants and eighteen police constables. One sergeant and six constables were on duty for Muswell Hill, as explained by Bernard Brown in *Hornsey Historical Society Bulletin No. 29* (1988). In 1904 Muswell Hill got its own station, in Fortis Green. Costing £5,570 it had stabling for six horses. Despite threats of closure and restricted hours it still operates 95 years later.

37. St James's church in the 1980s

Chapter 7

Muswell Hill becomes
a Community

How did the residents get to know each other? Religious allegiance was strong and churches could knit people together within their denomination once churches and church halls were built. Schools helped to bring parents together, and tennis, bowls, golf and other sporting clubs thrived. The Athenaeum offered social meeting points of various kinds. When and how did churches and other community centres arrive?

St James's had been the Church of England place of worship since its foundation in 1842 with the original structure extended in 1874 as attendance increased. In 1896 a church council was formed to consider what steps should be taken to provide for the growing parish. Church architect J S Alder was called in but virtually condemned the decaying building, a view endorsed by a second architect. A new church to accommodate 900 to 1,000 worshippers, 'built on improved and modern principles' was decided upon at a public meeting and J S Alder won the competition for its design. Fund raising ensued, starting with a bazaar in the large hall of St James's school where parishioners staged a musical tragedy called '*What You Will or The Villainous Squire, the Frivolous Friar and the Maid of Muswell Hill*'. The Maid of Muswell Hill was played by Miss Kathlee M Berton. I first heard the name 'Maid of Muswell' when it was chosen for a new public house on the corner of Alexandra Park Road and Grosvenor Road in the 1990s. I doubt if the lady who suggested the name then had heard of it either, for it seems to have been an obscure drama lost in the ephemera of history. (My entry for the pub-naming competition was 'The Rhodes' in memory of the owner of the nearby Tottenham Wood Farmhouse but it got nowhere!)

Fund raising was successful and the new St James's church was consecrated in 1901 but it was not completed with its tower and spire until 1910. Its location is 337 feet above sea level. The top of the spire is 179 feet high so that it has become a notable addition to the townscape and can be seen from a great distance. By 1911 a site in Fortis Green Road for a church hall had been secured but, with the intervention of the First World War, this was not built until 1925.

A survey of London worship with 400 well-supervised enumerators, was taken in 1903 for the nonconformists by Richard Mudie Smith and the *Daily News*. Out of London's population of 6,240,336 a fifth attended church; 538,477 Anglican, 545,317 nonconformist and 96,281 Roman Catholic. The congregations recorded for St James's church in 1903 were 677 to the morning service and 419 for evensong.

The size of St James's congregations can be compared with those for the nonconformist churches at Muswell Hill. The Congregationalists were as high, with 603 in the morning and 568 in the evening. Presbyterians, 489 in the morning and 328 in the evening. Methodists 349 in the morning and 305 in the evening. Baptists 314 in the morning and 370 in the evening. In 1903 on an average Sunday the total for nonconformist attendance in Muswell Hill was greater than that for the Church of England: 1096 for one C of E church compared with 3,326 for the four nonconformist churches. These statistics suggest that the religious affiliations of the new residents arriving in a suburb still being constructed were already well established.

The four nonconformist churches were all built as the new terraced houses were being erected. They often sprung from embryo congregations which existed before the splendid new buildings were put up. The Congregationalists, for example, after worshipping in the Muswell Hill drawing room of a Holborn solicitor, secured a Tetherdown site opposite Pages Lane for an iron church in 1891, that is, before the new suburb was built, with an established church congregation which embraced Baptists as well. Unfortunately this new Union church was weakened by personality clashes.

Revival came with Edmondson's donation of the present Congregational (now United Reformed) church site on the corner of Queens Avenue and Tetherdown in 1897, with building begun in 1898 to the designs of Percy Richard Morley Horder (1870-1944). The architect was the son of William Horder, Congregational Minister at Wood Green (whose name can be seen on the foundation stone of the Sunday School built behind the Congregational Chapel erected in 1864 in Lordship Lane and saved from demolition in 1998). Young Horder was only 28 when he designed the Muswell Hill Congregational Church; he dressed stylishly in cape and broad hat but was said to be puritan in character. He was to build other congregational churches in Leyton, Hackney, and Bowes Park. Muswell Hill opened for public service on May Day 1900 though a formal consecration ceremony had been performed in May 1899.

Like the Church of England the Congregationalists had to wait until after the First World War for a church hall. It was designed by Stanley Griffiths, architect and church member and built in 1928-29 opposite the church; it has recently been listed. The church itself has fine acoustics and has been used for music concerts. From the beginning it was a meeting-point for newcomers, many wealthy from trade such as Edwin Unwin, brother of publisher Stanley Unwin and partner in the printing firm of Unwin Brothers. It was a vital point in the formation of the new community.

The Presbyterians were quick to acquire a site from Edmondson soon after he bought the Fortis House and Limes estate in 1896. The Church Extension Committee of the London Presbytery (which had built a church in 1887 in Highgate) became aware of this development and in 1897 Sir George Barclay Bruce, the convenor of the committee, purchased this central site out of his own money. He leased it to the newly formed congregation for a nominal sum and advanced the money for the building of a church hall which would serve as a temporary church. Designs for this were obtained from Arthur O Breeds with building begun in the spring of 1898, soon after the shops in Edmondson's first parades were opened. The plain brick Gothic style building in Princes Avenue opened in November 1898. The congregation having thus been established, a minister was appointed, and fund raising for a new church began. Sales of work were organised by Muswell Hill people which were augmented by a marathon three-day bazaar where the amusements offered included a ladies nail-driving competition, a recital on an Edison Grand Concert Phonograph and a trained American duck.

Arthur O Breeds was among the five architects selected to enter designs for the new Presbyterian church, along with Thomas Arnold, Archibald Dickie and George Lethbridge. But the winner was the firm of George and Reginald Baines who had recently designed the Baptist Church in Dukes Avenue, formally opened in 1902. George Baines (1852-1934) articled in Great Yarmouth, won a competition to build a Baptist chapel in Accrington where he set up his practice till moving to London in 1884. In 1901 he took his son Reginald into the practice and designed over 200 church and school buildings as well as blocks of flats in Westminster, also stores, factories and a model village for Messrs. Chivers & Sons.

The delightful Broadway church, described as 'the nose on the face of Muswell Hill' is in Art Nouveau Gothic, built with white flints and hard Ruabon brick with a tower (with spirelet) to turn the corner into Princes Avenue. Baines was to repeat the design in the Braemar Avenue Baptist Chapel (off Bounds Green Road) of 1907. The fine interior of the Broadway church with raked, semi-circular seating, was designed to accommodate about a thousand people. The foundation stone is 1902 and the church opened in 1903. The Breeds building at the rear was then used as the church hall.

The Baines building can be appreciated because it is positioned almost directly opposite Hillfield Park, making it possible to look at it from a distance. One can only speculate whether Edmondson had this in mind when he sold that particular site to Sir George Barclay Bruce, or when he positioned the line of Hillfield Park up to the Broadway over the Hillfield estate. At all events it is an excellent corner site on the Broadway for the church.

All the nonconformist churches in Muswell Hill were to be built on corners except perhaps the Baptists who built as near the top end of planned Dukes Avenue as Edmondson would allow. But the Congregational church stands on the corner of Queens Avenue and Tetherdown, the Presbyterians on Princes Avenue corner and the Wesleyan Methodists was built on the corner of Colney Hatch Lane with Alexandra Park Road (though it has now gone). This accorded with new nonconformist thinking. Architects Joseph Crouch and Edmund Butler in a 1901 book about buildings for nonconformists argue that 'the time for building...in back streets has gone by....Non-conformity is now a power in the land....it is hardly necessary to point out the importance of choosing the site for the New Church in a leading thoroughfare....If possible a corner site should be chosen....The lighting is more easily managed, besides the other important advantage of a commanding position'. The authors also argued that they were not to be weak copies of Anglican models; the ideal was a modified form of Gothic. Baines's church for the Presbyterians in particular fulfills these design criteria. Part of its impact is due to the use of bright red Ruabon brick. Originally he intended to use a light yellow brick with terracotta dressings from Costessey near Norwich but delivery problems led him to the Welsh brick instead.

This is perhaps the moment to mention the fate of this splendid building. In 1972 the Presbyterians and Congregationalists in Muswell Hill amalgamated to form a United Reform Church and it was decided to use the Congregational church and sell the Presbyterian one. Local protests led to a 1978 Department of the Environment Enquiry leading to the Grade II listed building being saved from demolition. Plans to make it into a concert hall failed. Ultimately it was leased by Haringey council as offices but not found satisfactory by its housing staff. After standing empty it was converted in 1997 into a pub with a brewery on the premises, the 'Fantail and Firkin', the Fantail being a reference to local pigeons. So popular is it that it has to have bouncers in the evenings, enough to make Presbyterians turn in their graves. The hall behind has been converted into flats.

Creation of a Baptist church was due in good measure to the Reverend W J Mills, Vice-President of the London Baptist Association and in due course the first Muswell Hill pastor. The Association thought accommodation should be provided at Muswell Hill and Mills went with another pastor 'to spy out the land'. Seeing an Edmondson hoarding on the Dukes Avenue site they called on Edmondson at his Queens Avenue office and Edmondson generously agreed to donate a site. First he offered them the corner of Colney Hatch Lane and Muswell Road but Mr Mills wanted a more central site. So Edmondson offered them the site of the old Elms mansion in what is now Dukes Avenue, which they gladly accepted.

Mills gathered a committee of local Baptists and the other major developer W J Collins donated £200 to the cost. George Baines was selected as architect and suggested that, as the site was sloping and the church had to be built on piers, they should go deeper to provide space for class rooms under the church. Seating for about 750 was provided with a gallery which, at Mr Mills's request, was curved instead of being straight-fronted so that it was in the style of Queens Hall, where Sir Henry Wood's Promenade concerts were held, in Portland Place. The new congregation met meanwhile in Norfolk House school in Muswell Avenue, membership increasing.

Mrs Edmondson laid the foundation stone in July 1901, on her birthday, and those taking part adjourned to Fortismere where W J Collins gave a garden party. In 1902 the church opened, adding another fine building to Muswell Hill, its little tower with 'spike' adding to the townscape. The red brick building is another Baines excursion into a free adaptation of Perpendicular Gothic style and its interior retains its charm.

The church helped create a community by manifold activities, including a literary society (which held a joint debate with the Presbyterian Literary Society on the subject of Women's Suffrage in 1907), a Ladies' Working Meeting, boy scouts and girl guides who used the popular church gymnasium on separate evenings, a Sunday School with 190 belonging, a Young People's Society of Christian Endeavour and the Girls' Guild of Help aimed mainly at girls in domestic service.

Wesleyans were to have their church in Colney Hatch Lane, on the corner with Alexandra Park Road, opened in April 1899. Methodists had met before this in private houses, such as Essex View in Colney Hatch Lane (the 1840s villa now called Alabama which at one time had views across to Essex hills) or in Tottenham Wood House, the former farmhouse owned by the Alexandra Palace company, whose occupant William Russell was one of the company's bailiffs. They were granted use for one shilling a month of the Norwegian Chalet, one of the Palace and Park exhibition buildings which stood at the foot of the present day road called The Avenue then an entrance road through the park to the palace. Methodist worshiped here from 1891 till the new church was ready.

Built on a site bought for £400 from Mr E N Gill a builder, designed by architect Josiah Gunton, a Methodist, the church took five years to build before final completion with a corner tower and chancel. An adjacent Sunday School building by architect Arthur Boney was built soon after; many might remember the side wall bricks carrying the initials of the children who had donated to its cost. The Sunday School pioneered grading and proved to be a successful institution over the years. Before the Sunday School was built the Methodists had erected in 1901 the Iron Hall which the Congregationalists had previously used in Tetherdown, the gift of Mr Hughes of Fairfield, Tetherdown. This now redundant structure was then set up in Pembroke Road, on the north side of Muswell Hill, to act as a Mission Hall; it survived on the site until the 1990s.

Although they were well established in Finchley there was no provision for Roman Catholics in Muswell Hill until the Edwardian era. In 1903 an order of nuns of St Martin de Tours had been effectively forced to leave France (with other Catholic teaching orders) and was encouraged by the Finchley parish priest, Father Powell, to come to Muswell Hill. They settled first at Newport Villa in Tetherdown (now used by Haringey Education Department) where Mass was attended by some forty or fifty Catholics and then moved in 1907 to Springfield House in Pages Lane which became their Convent and where Mass could be heard in the hall of the school which the nuns opened.

In 1917 Father Powell moved into a Colney Hatch Lane villa called Oncot which stood opposite where the nuns' farm had been in the Middle Ages. A temporary church was built in 1920 at the rear then the house was demolished so that the present Our Lady of Muswell church could be built. This was completed in 1938 but in 1928 Father Powell himself had died, the dampness and decay of Oncot, the old villa, being suspected of contributing to his early death aged 60. The convent continued in Springfield House, extended as the private school flourished, but since 1981 it has been occupied by the Sisters of Marie Auxiliatrice. From 1959 the school became part of the state system for infants and juniors with additional buildings. A flourishing social life accompanies church activities and Our Lady of Muswell Hill Tennis Club has its own premises and courts in Rhodes Avenue.

38. The Athenaeum in Fortis Green Road photographed in 1963 shortly before its demolition; Sainsbury now occupy the site.

39. The Muswell Hill Parliament photographed in 1908; this debating society used to meet in The Athenaeum; it survived till the 1950s.

The Society of Friends, or Quakers, also had a building in Muswell Hill from a later date. Their meetings were held at the Athenaeum but in 1926 a meeting house was built by them in Church Crescent. This building has been usefully hired by other organisations, especially since Muswell Hill lost the Athenaeum in 1966.

The Athenaeum was a focal point for Muswell Hill life for over sixty years. Edmondson reserved a site for it between St James's Parade and Princes Parade and from 1900 erected a classical building with pediment and two domed towers with rusticated arched frontage onto the street with a glass canopy. Inside were two halls, seating 466 and 200 respectively and many other rooms. It was used at different times for a conservatoire of music, a girls' school (from 1910), a cinema (from 1920) and for a debating society called the Muswell Hill Parliament which lasted many decades. It was also used for religious purposes, not only by the Society of Friends but also by a spiritualist church and for a synagogue. A street-front shop was occupied by a commercial photographer. My personal memory of it is going there for a jumble sale before its 1966 demolition. In Edwardian times the name Athenaeum was more familiar, as it was given to several literary or scientific institution buildings; the most famous survivor is the gentleman's club off Pall Mall built in 1830 by architect Decimus Burton. The name derives from the Greek word for the temple of Athene, goddess of wisdom. The demolition at Muswell Hill occurred before conservation legislation was brought in and only the corner building survives leading into the cul-de-sac called Athenaeum Place. The Athenaeum was replaced by a block of flats with Sainsbury's supermarket at ground level.

An entertainments building which I never saw was the Summerland Theatre. This stood at the end of Summerland Gardens and is primarily remembered by older people as a cinema which vanished from the scene soon after, in 1936, Muswell Hill acquired Ritz and Odeon cinemas. It seems to have begun in the tradition of the pleasure garden such as at Vauxhall, Highbury Barn or Cremorne. A surviving September 1913 brochure offers different programmes of music for Thursday, Friday and Saturday whilst in the theatre on Thursday films were being shewn, including a Vitagraph Drama called *His Life for His Emperor* and the comedy *The Heart of a Doll*. An advertisement in the *Muswell Hill Record* of April 1916 shows the 'Muswell Hill Electric Theatre' offering 'Hall Caine's masterpiece *The Eternal City*' three times daily at 3, 5.30 and 8 pm, with prices of admission at one shilling, sixpence and three pence (old coinage) and children under 12 half price. Also being shown on other days were two 'Official War Films', *Ypres* and *The Prince of Wales in the Front Line*. Coming soon was Mary Pickford in *Mistress Nell* in four parts. Seats could be booked in advance at no extra charge. The garden seems to have occupied the hilly slope now used for a car park, and to have been lit in the evening with thousands of fairy lights. Inclusive admission to the gardens and theatre in 1913 was sixpence. This land was originally part of the Summerland estate but presumably Finnane found it too hilly to build on easily. The slope is painfully obvious for some of the elderly who make their way to Muswell Hill's only public toilet open in 1999, placed in the car park in the 1980s.

Alexandra Palace and Park could also be said to have followed in the old pleasure garden tradition as regards entertainments, including fireworks, balloonists, rope walkers and educational displays, all activities there in Edwardian years. With public ownership in 1900 improved access via two tram routes and increased leisure time, the

Palace and Park passed through a comparatively prosperous period up to the First World War, especially from 1910 under Alderman Edwin Sloper's chairmanship of the trustees. Film shows were given from 1911 to 1914 and actually made a profit. Crowds came to see Dolly Shepherd, a girl who had got a waitress job at the palace to hear the American musician Souza play but had been taken on as a lady parachutist by Captain Auguste Gaudron, a French aeronaut who provided aeronautical displays. Dolly, garbed in a suitable self-designed knickerbocker suit, ascended in a balloon and came down by parachute, a career she followed with great success across the country from 1903 to 1912, despite accidents and her making a dramatic mid-air rescue of another lady parachutist who got into difficulties.

The usually dismal fortunes of the Palace have intrigued all Muswell Hill residents ever since; mostly people have been concerned with keeping the 200 acre park free of encumbrances in recent years, so that they can enjoy its natural beauty. More parkland was released when the racecourse, which opened in the park in 1868, closed down in 1970 after the Jockey Club declared it not up to standard. But the building secured another claim to fame when in 1936 the world's first regular high definition television service was inaugurated here by the BBC, an achievement which many do not seem to appreciate. Nor is it widely known that Robert Paul opened the UK's first film studio in Sydney Road on the north side of Muswell Hill in 1899.

Television was unknown to the Edwardians and to later generations until it began to be seen widely in the 1950s and 1960s. It should also be remembered that the Edwardian era did not have the radio as an entertainment either. The Literary Society founded in 1901 at the Methodist church at Muswell Hill claimed its members to be among the first people in the world to hear an actual wireless broadcast without the use of earphones. This was after the end of the First World War when the chief engineer of the British Broadcasting Company brought electrical gear and reproduced music transmitted by a friend in London. We take radio today for granted, like tap water, but it originated only within my own generation. I remember as a small child in the late 1920s sitting in my grandparents' home with earphones whilst my grandfather moved a wire on a small piece of crystal so that I could pick up a radio broadcast. Soon after I was listening to Uncle Mac and Children's Hour on a proper radio fitted with valves; transistors and portable radios were a long way ahead, as was miniaturisation.

For many then, and now, relaxation was the feel of a glass in the hand, and social company in the ambience of a public house. But Edwardian Muswell Hill saw the Temperance movement holding sway. Edmondson had wanted to build a licensed hotel on the corner of Queens Avenue and Fortis Green Road and he designed and built an impressive, pillared corner building for this site. But Temperance opposition thwarted him, annoyingly led by the Congregationalists, to whom he had given the site opposite for their new church. No public house was provided by Collins either, so Muswell Hill men (well, I suppose women might have wanted to go too, but it was not considered 'respectable' for ladies to enter pubs), seeking to go out for a convivial hour had the choice of either The Green Man or the tiny Royal Oak, which was the meeting point for villagers living nearby, or they could go to the Clissold Arms or The Alexandra in Fortis Green. Perhaps the club which opened at Princes Avenue (which survived until 1999) was one answer for the thirsty man who wanted to go out for a drink.

40. Edmondson intended the building on the left, on the corner of Queens Avenue and Fortis Green Road, to be a licensed hotel but was defeated by the temperance movement; Collins has yet to build Birchwood Mansions on the right in this view.

41. Temperance movement opposition prevented the building of public houses in the Edwardian suburb; The John Baird in Fortis Green Road was built in 1959 on the bombed corner of Fortis Green Road and Princes Avenue. Baird provided trial television programmes for the BBC at nearby Alexandra Palace in 1936.

Men with political interest found attendance at Muswell Hill Parliament a satisfying opportunity to stand up and express views. This now forgotten society was one of at least a dozen in the country (another was Hampstead) which followed the procedures of the House of Commons to debate political issues. In the 1920-21 session, for example, it debated 'the excessive rates in local boroughs', measures for dealing with unemployment, the appointment of a Public Defender, and proportional representation. Members represented constituencies, had party allegiances and were supervised by a Speaker and there was a mace. It had originated in 1908 and met originally in the Athenaeum, later the Presbyterian hall, then in Tollington school hall where it was televised by the BBC from Alexandra Palace in 1948. But interest was to wane and it ceased to meet in the 1950s. Probably like the outdoor political meeting (at Spouters Corner, Wood Green for example) it was a casualty of communication changes where political debate shifted from packed local halls to the national television screen or radio broadcast.

The parliament was predominantly a male preserve, I suspect, and women would have had their own groups especially those attached to the churches. They would also have socialised among the many small shops that graced the new suburb and would have travelled to the West End to visit the department stores: Whiteleys, Harrods, Dickens & Jones, Marshall & Snellgrove, Swan & Edgar, Debenham & Freebody, Liberty's, the Army & Navy, the Civil Service Stores, John Lewis, Arthur Gamage, Burberry's, Waring & Gillow, John Maple, and from 1906 Selfridge's, all of which offered delights in rebuilt Edwardian stores. Jones brothers of Holloway was nearer, and delivered to Muswell Hill.

Muswell Hill ladies would have been concerned with finding servants; many of the larger houses had rooms designed for a live-in maid and butlers are also remembered. A 1916 issue of the *Muswell Hill Record* contains twelve small advertisements seeking domestic help. It was the Second World War which made servants scarce, a change from which middle class social life never fully recovered, and the servants' rooms were adapted to other purposes.

In those days, generally speaking, women did not go out to work after marriage (it was customary to resign on marriage, except in wartime) and the upbringing of children was often their chief concern, including finding suitable schools. In Victorian times Muswell Hill had had only one infant and junior school, that of St James's; a state school for younger children was not provided until 1913, and then the building in Alexandra Place was 'temporary' (known as the tin school to Teresa when she taught there and as the tinpot school to the pupils); the site was still in school use in the 1970s.

Middle class residents looked for a private school and there were plenty of these across the borough, and many in Muswell Hill, catering both for younger and older pupils. Norfolk House School for juniors had been built in 1897 in Muswell Avenue and in 1908 claimed to be the only purpose-built school out of 17 then existing. The school also catered for older girls and had a School of Domestic Science at 11 Alexandra Park Road where boarders were received. Other private schools included the Brakespeare House Day and Boarding School for Girls at 30 Muswell Road; Highfield Day and Boarding School for Boys, and the Cranley House Day and

Boarding School for Girls, both in Muswell Hill Road; and also nearby Kings House School for Girls (run by Miss Lear whose pupils were known as Cordelians.) There was a Modern School for Girls and Kindergarten at 2 Queens Avenue (established 1898), the St Margaret School for Girls at 11, Queens Avenue, and others.

Secondary education might involve attendance at church schools such as St Aloysius for Catholics in Highgate, or the prestigious Stationers' School in Crouch End founded by the City livery company of the same name. Provision came to Muswell Hill when in 1902 a branch of Tollington School (on the Islington/Stroud Green border) was opened in Tetherdown. This was built by William Campbell Brown, son of the school founder and joint proprietor, in the front garden of his set-back villa, Thorntons, in Tetherdown. I was a frequent attender of adult education classes run by the council and by the Workers Educational Association in this tall red brick, rather gaunt building and was always intrigued by the vestiges of the original house which could be identified at the rear, inside and out. Today the building is used by Fortismere comprehensive school which occupies a large site behind it carved out of the remains of Hornsey Common and Coldfall Woods (there still remains a large stretch of open space occupied by playing fields here).

Tollington was a boys' school, to be bought in 1919 by Middlesex County Council and developed as a proud grammar school, where local historian F M W Draper was to be headmaster. Similar provision was made for girls when Tollington Girls School was opened in 1911 in Grand Avenue; this was taken over in 1958 for Tetherdown infant and junior school (where Teresa was to teach for a dozen years).

Kings House School for Girls in Muswell Hill Road, mentioned above, stayed in a house called Cranley Dene until 1939 when it was evacuated. The building (and the house next to it) became a home for the blind but when it moved away the two old Victorian villas were demolished by Haringey council and replaced by the 1980s buildings also named Cranley Dene. Highfield school nearby survived until 1925.

Another long established institution was the Muswell Hill Cottage Home for Girls, based in Pages Lane, dating from the 1880s which housed about a dozen children whose mothers had died or abandoned their children on remarriage or had other problems. It was well supported as a charity by the Free Churches of Muswell Hill; the home was unsectarian but the children attended St James's, a practice started from the home's foundation by Mrs Percival Hart of Highgate.

Muswell Hill students would have needed to travel to Highgate for a public lending library until 1931. The Highgate Library had been opened in 1902 with 400 volumes and had been designed by council engineer Edwin J Lovegrove. Under Libraries legislation local councils could decide whether to spend rates on library provision and one point of view was that richer areas should not be provided with free loan books at the expense of the less well off. So although Edmondson had given a site for a public library opposite the Baptist church he withdrew it in 1910 when it became obvious that the council was not going to build one. Finally it was built in 1931 on the former fire station site in Queens Avenue. Meanwhile Muswell Hill residents would have had to rely on private lending libraries for their books, such as The Royal Library operating at 18 Queens Parade; more national provision was by Mudie's and by the lending libraries set up by Boots the Chemists in their chains of shops and by W H Smith (a provision which survived till the 1950s when the cheap availability of paperbacks rendered them uneconomic).

Some older people instead of reading went bowling instead, using the Muswell Hill Bowling Club facilities for which Edmondson had provided land between Kings Avenue (where the entrance is) Queens Avenue and Tetherdown. Or, if they could afford the fees they joined the Muswell Hill Golf Club, using the old Tottenham Wood farmhouse as its clubhouse and a social venue. Young people went roller skating at the rink in Alexandra Palace, a popular venue for the major part of the twentieth century. For most of the young these and other delights were to end after 1914 when war took so many away, as it was again in the Second World War. But the Palace roller skating rink continued to operate throughout the 1939-45 war and continued to flourish for many years afterwards till the 1970s when it was closed for repairs and never reopened.

Chapter 8

Muswell Hill in Later Years

The suburb created by Edmondson with the aid of Collins and other builders remained remarkably untouched during the twentieth century. Empty sites were filled and development continued in Fortis Green. In the 1920s Billy Collins built the block of flats called Fortis Court on the corner with Fortis Green Road, then Woodside, a similar block on the corner with Tetherdown, both to my eye quite pleasing in design.

More radical change took place from the 1920s when Coldfall Wood was largely eliminated. North of Creighton Avenue Hornsey sought to remedy the shortage of council housing by laying out the Coldfall estate, a grid of five roads with 412 terraced houses, erected 1924-25, supported by a council school for seniors, juniors and infants opened in 1928. The Church of England, with the aid of the Missionary Society, built a wooden mission hall in 1925 on the corner of Creighton Avenue and Coppetts Road, replaced in 1940 by the plain brick church of St Matthew. (In the 1980s this site was redeveloped for housing). Fortunately 34 remaining acres of woods were acquired by the council and remain usable open space stretching north towards later playing fields and to the large cemetery (where Teresa is buried) now bounded on its north side by the North Circular Road, constructed in the late 1920s. This is the effective boundary of both built up Muswell Hill and of the old Hornsey parish, where Finchley/Hornsey common once stretched.

Between Creighton Avenue and Fortis Green further building took place in the 1930s, Collins building blocks of flats with elegant iron balconies called Long Ridges in 1930 and just east of these the two blocks of Twyford Court flats in 1933. These Twyford Court blocks lie each side of Twyford Avenue, which has houses built by Collins in the style of his Rookfield garden suburb, with tile-hung gabled roofs; this attractive enclave benefits from proximity to the unbuilt upon green spaces of Fortismere school's playing fields, from which views north can be obtained.

Fortis Green saw further building after the Second World War including the 1947 Keynes Close, a pleasant quadrangle of elderly people's bungalows off Annington Road, and Blaenavon on the bombed corner of Western Road. (The Midhurst Gardens in Fortis Green were made slightly larger when a German flying bomb demolished 1 to 4 Cheapside (Collins's row of shops) in July 1944; unfortunately two were killed and 16 injured in this bombing).

Other new buildings in Muswell Hill in the 1920s and 1930s included the St James's Church hall erected in Fortis Green Road in 1925 to the designs of George Grey Wornum (who was to build the Royal Institute of British Architects headquarters in Portland Place) and in 1928 Tetherdown Hall. This was the period when blocks of flats began to be more acceptable generally but not to Hornsey council which saw them as unwelcome in the area. A battle was fought over plans to build Dorchester Court in Colney Hatch Lane, on the corner of Muswell Road but the flats were finally agreed, limited to four storeys, in 1927. This was the beginning of the demolition of the old Colney Hatch Lane villas with their replacement in the 1930s by blocks of flats called Barrington Court, St Ivian Court, Cedar Court and Seymour Court, on sites north of Pages Lane. One of the last to go was Thatched House, a thatched survival just past the petrol station where a resident later recalled 'The girls used to ride out on their horses for a gentle trot along a much quieter (Colney Hatch) Lane'.

I remember Essex Lodge which survived here till the late 1950s when it was replaced by a block with same name. Here Harriet Rhodes once lived, daughter of the family which had owned Tottenham Wood Farm. Local historian F M W Draper in his booklet *Muswell Rhymes* wrote:

'At Essex Lodge, his daughter dear,
Miss Harriet resided,
A lady of appearance queer
And notions most decided.
When Cecil Rhodes to Muswell hied,
Desisting from his labours,
Miss Harriet showed him off with pride
To all the friends and neighbours'.

Local resident Mrs Sylvia Hodgson recalled that in the 1920s Colney Hatch Lane was indeed a more truly country lane before it was widened:

'Then the old buses would stop anywhere at the wave of a hand or a ring on the bell cord. Tradesmen's entrances on the side gates were the norm for all houses then. My mother ordered and had almost everything delivered and the front door was never used for the receipt of deliveries or for dealing with tradesmen. Muswell Hill was then known as 'Church-going Muswell Hill'. 'Our behaviour was always to uphold the tone of the school (Tollington High School for Girls). We were not allowed to walk more than two abreast or arm-in-arm nor to eat sweets in the street'.

A modern building arrived in 1937 in Pages Lane when the 1861 almshouses were replaced by Whitehall Court. This tall, white block is in the 'international modern' architectural style of the time, echoing Highpoint, the celebrated block of flats built at Highgate. But east of it part of rural Muswell Hill remains in the shape of North Bank. This and the Grove Lodge estate are the only two survivors from the earlier Muswell Hill. North Bank's survival was largely due to Lloyd's underwriter Harold Guylee Chester (1887-1973) who bought it in 1924 and by 1932 had seen through alterations to the house to make it available to the Methodist church as a centre for youth. In subsequent years North Bank has played an important role in Muswell Hill not only for its own Methodist work but as a venue for social events arranged by voluntary organisations.

Guy Chester owned the surviving villas in Colney Hatch Lane and No. 7 (called Hazelhyrst) is now used by the Methodists for various activities. No. 9 (Devonhire Lodge) was demolished in the 1950s by Chester who paid for the erection here of Chester House, used as Methodist church offices and as a youth hostel. Built 1959-60 in pale brick to designs by architect Charles Pike it makes an acceptable, large addition to the Colney Hatch Lane corner. In 1984 a new church was added onto the North Bank house, designed by Peter Knollt and Chris Lelliot. It replaced the 1899 church in Colney Hatch Lane which had to be given up due to cracking; flats named Caroline Close now occupy the site on the corner of Alexandra Park Road.

The year 1936 saw great changes. As well as the disappearance of the Victorian almshouses the Post Office in Colney Hatch Lane was rebuilt and two cinemas arrived. The Odeon was built on the corner of Fortis Green Road and Muswell Hill Road, replacing houses. Odeon though a name indicating a Greek theatre was popularly taken to stand for 'Oscar Deutsch Entertains Our Nation', for he was the man who built the chain of Odeon cinemas across the country in the 1930s. Originally it was intended to have its entrance in Muswell Hill Road but opposition from St James's church opposite led to this being skewed round at right angles. The cinema is regarded as the masterpiece of architect George Coles and is listed Grade II starred, mainly for the beauty of its preserved Art Deco interior. The cinema is part of a parade of shops and flats, with a large car park at the rear where the former houses had their gardens.

The Odeon opened in September 1936 and the Ritz cinema in December 1936 on a site opposite The Green Man previously occupied by shops. This was a well designed building by cinema architect W R Glen. From 1962 it was the ABC and I remember many visits to its pleasant interior. Demolished in 1978 it was replaced by a tall brick office block, the design of which was improved by the intervention of the local Conservation Area Advisory Committee.

The new cinemas represented the entertainment fashion which swept across the suburbs and the country between the wars, with large, purpose-built auditoriums accommodating thousands. The loss of the Ritz in Muswell Hill was the reverse of the boom, with television supplanting cinema as the entertainment screen in post Second World War years. The demolition of cinemas was also aided by the boom in supermarkets, the now fashionable form of shopping which resulted from spread of motor car use; these required suitable sites in shopping areas before they later began

42. The Express Dairy tea room, the White House and the ABC cinema are to be seen on the right. On the left between the BSM shop and The Green Man is one of Muswell Hill's oldest buildings, now a cafe.

43. Lyons tea rooms in Muswell Hill Broadway used the post-war self-service system. Photographed in August 1962 it closed a month later.

to be built further out where land for car parking was also available. This movement led to the demolition of halls such as the Athenaeum, a loss that is still felt in Muswell Hill which lacks good halls. In 1999 the Odeon at Muswell Hill was one of only two cinemas open in the Borough of Haringey, though two multiplexes being built in nearby Wood Green reflect a new cinema boom. Frequented by Muswell Hill residents over the years has been the 1910 cinema in East Finchley now called the Phoenix.

Another 1930s building was the public library in Queens Avenue, designed by Borough Architect W H Adams and opened in 1931. It was listed in the 1990s partly because of the murals upstairs painted by the Hornsey College of Art. Another council building is Vallette Court, built in 1934 in St James's Lane, but this is unlikely to be listed. It replaced the 26 old cottages dating back to rural times. Many old buildings were removed from St James's Lane in the 1920s and 1930s in 'improvement' schemes by the council.

Destruction occurred during the Second World War with bombs in Collingwood Avenue, Leaside Avenue, Firs Avenue, Fortis Green Road, Princes Avenue, Queens Avenue and elsewhere. The chief casualty was probably St James's church burnt out by a fire bomb on 19th April 1941, but restored after the war. The bomb on the end of St James's Parade allowed a public house to be built on the corner with Princes Avenue in 1959, which might have gladdened the heart of Edmondson. This was named The John Baird after the television pioneer whose work was put to the test at Alexandra Palace in 1936. Although successful transmissions were made by the Baird system, that by Marconi-EMI, tried at the same time, was eventually chosen, enabling world changes in entertainment.

The steam railway line to the Palace closed for passengers in 1954 and this allowed the building of an Infant and Junior school on the former track bed in the 1960s. In 1958 in Tetherdown a four-storey block was built at the rear of Tollington Boys' School and became a new mixed-sex grammar school called simply Tollington School, which, merging with the William Grimshaw secondary modern school in Creighton Avenue became Creighton comprehensive school in 1965. In 1983, with falling school rolls, this amalgamated with Alexandra Park comprehensive school and was renamed Fortismere School. In 1965 next to the first Tollington school in Tetherdown the Muswell Hill Synagogue was built.

The 'school run' has with the spread of car ownership become a feature of our everyday life where children are brought to school in a vehicle instead of walking as they did until the later 1970s. The growth of car ownership and of motorised transport of all kinds has probably brought the greatest physical change to Muswell Hill's otherwise still Edwardian-shaped built environment. Congestion, parking, and exhaust fumes are some of the disadvantages that this convenient form of transport has brought with it, but the other effect is the arrival of traffic lights, mini-roundabouts, road humps, traffic islands, pedestrian crossings and road markings, transforming those placid scenes depicted in Edwardian picture postcards where people casually stroll in the road. Whilst the Edwardian shopping parades (despite some nasty shopfronts) and residential avenues largely retain their charm, the roads themselves are no longer what they were. Nevertheless the Muswell Hill Partnership

Scheme between Haringey Council and English Heritage, with a lottery money grant and council funding has been finding ways to restore Edwardian environmental features to the Broadway, including a possible revamping of the roundabout. The scheme was expected to cost nearly half a million pounds over three years.

What is the economic composition of Muswell Hill? Has it changed in recent years? A council social survey report in 1984 stated:

> 'Only one third of Muswell Hill's residents work within the borough, with the majority commuting elsewhere. Car transport is used by 40 per cent of people travelling to work...Muswell Hill had very little industry other than a few, small craft and light industrial concerns such as printing and clothing manufacture...most local employment is within shops, offices and local government including education and civic amenities.' 'The 1981 Census tells us that Muswell Hill district is favoured by the self-employed and supervisory economic groups and by immigrants from countries other than the New Commonwealth. The total population of the district is approximately 29,000.'

One controversial recommendation was provision in the centre of open space for play areas for mothers and toddlers, and others. This was received with scepticism. Another was to discourage conversion of larger houses into flats because it brought increased car pressure. This was in the context of Muswell Hill being designated a Conservation Area where buildings cannot be demolished or external alterations made without planning permission.

In recent decades Muswell Hill personalities have come to world prominence. In pop music Rod Stewart, a local boy, bought his (late) mother a house in Colney Hatch Lane. The group known as The Kinks, brothers Ray and Dave Davies, who attended Creighton School, first performed in the 1960s in The Clissold Arms in Fortis Green, opposite their family home in Denmark Terrace. Their first gig was held in the Athenaeum. Items about the guitar-playing brothers and song writers are to be seen in The Clissold Arms. Earlier the film star Peter Sellers lived circa 1960 at 72 Tetherdown, the first house he owned. He had lived between 1936 and 1939 at a cottage in Muswell Hill Road (near Archway Road) which now has a plaque. Actors and other media people have moved into Muswell Hill in recent years and faces well-known from film or television are to be seen. One of them, Maureen Lipman, has featured living in Muswell Hill in her humorous books.

Well known for a murder in 1896, Muswell Hill was to become similarly notorious in recent times. In 1983 a Haringey council worker called to deal with a blocked drain at a Cranley Gardens house uncovered human remains. As a result Denis Nilson was sentenced to life imprisonment for six murders carried out between 1979 and 1983. Opposite Muswell Hill roundabout is a small memorial, garlanded with flowers, dedicated to local policeman P C Keith Blakelock who died in October 1985 in the riots at Broadwater Farm, Tottenham. The Police Memorial Trust placed the memorial near the shop where he met his wife.

Some older local figures have passed on, such as Mrs Kearey who died in 1998 aged 94. In 1919 with her husband Ted she helped set up the Palmsville Garage in Colney Hatch Lane, a still thriving business which has increased the number of Rover cars being driven in Muswell Hill (including my own).

So generation succeeds generation: eighteenth century occupants are replaced by Victorians whose estates disappear to make room for more numerous Edwardians, and later generations. The twentieth century has ended with communications achievements which undermine the whole process of travelling to an office to work, on which the suburb has been largely based. But its period charm still attracts residents. The world is never still. No generation lasts for ever, change is always the order of the day, as this chronology has shewn. Many of us look back nostalgically to an ideal world we once lived in so as to escape perhaps our own current agonies and problems. But Muswell Hill the place will serve now and in the future in different ways, as yet we know not how.

ENVOI

Sources

Primary

Maps

1725   *A New and Correct Map of Middlesex*, Essex and Hertfordshire with the roads, rivers and sea coasts actually surveyed 1725 by John Warburton, Joseph Bland and Payler Smith. (British Library Map Room)

1754   *A Topographical Map of Middlesex* by John Rocque 1754 by Act of Parliament (reproduced by London & Middlesex Archaeological Society 1971).

1800   *Thomas Milne's Land Use Map of London & Environs in 1800* (reproduced by the London Topographical Society with an Introduction by G B G Bull 1975-76).

1816   Hornsey Enclosure Award and Map (London Metropolitan Archives)

1864   Ordnance Survey map of Muswell Hill 1:2500 1st edition (reproduced by HHS)

1894   Ordnance Survey map 1:2500 2nd edition (reproduced by HHS)

1913   Ordnance Survey map 1:2500 3rd edition (reproduced by HHS)

         Bomb Damage in the Borough of Hornsey 1939-45 (Bruce Castle Museum London N17) (BC).

Manorial Rolls

Hornsey Manor Court Rolls (Guildhall Library, City of London)

Court Rolls of the Bishop of London's Manor of Hornsey 1603-1701 by W McB & F Marcham (Grafton & Co. 1929). (HHS Archives)

Legal and Sales Documents

Deed of Covenant dated 15 December 1825 and later legal documents relating to The Limes estate at Muswell Hill (London Metropolitan Archives)

Sale Catalogue for The Elms: 5th August 1880 (British Library Map Room)

Auction Sale documents for Avenue House: 28th July 1885 and 13th May 1891 (BC)

Auction Sale document for Springfield House: 12th October 1906 (BC)

Auction Sale document for Rookfield House: 25th March 1912 (BC)

Abstract of Title of James Edmondson to freehold premises known as the Bowling Green, Muswell Hill 1902 (Muswell Hill Bowling Club)

Rate Books

Hornsey – various dates in nineteenth century (BC)

Clerkenwell Detached – 1850-1890 (Islington Local History Collection – Finsbury Library)

Census returns for Muswell Hill: 1841-1891 (Formerly History Centre, now at Family Public Record Office)

Newspapers and Directories

The Hornsey Journal and Finsbury Park Standard (HHS Archives)

The Muswell Hill Record (British Library, Colindale)

Kelly's *Directories of Hornsey*, annually 1880-1939 (Guildhall Library)

Local Authority Reports

Hornsey Urban District Council Review of the Years 1896-1900 (1900; HHS Archives)

Planning Committee Minutes of Hornsey UDC and Borough (Hornsey Library)

The Borough of Hornsey 1903-1953 (Hornsey Borough Council 1953) (HHS Archives)

The Odeon Cinema, Muswell Hill – Proposal for listing by D W Frith (BC)

Muswell Hill District Report 1984 by D W Frith (BC)

Department of the Environment Report

Enquiry into Appeals by the Presbyterian Church of England Trust under the Town and Country Planning Act 1971 re site of former Presbyterian church, Muswell Hill (December 1978) (BC)

Unpublished Studies

The Rookfield Estate – Observations on its History, Architecture and Conservation by Ivor Stilitz and David Frith (Rookfield Owners and Tenants Association 1977) (HHS Archives)]

The Records of the Clay Family by Mary Aimee Clay (1908) (Highgate LSI)

A Demographic Study of two localities in the Parish of Hornsey in 1851 by Jean Corker (Dissertation for B.Ed Part II at Trent Park, Middlesex Poly n.d.)

Factors which influenced the Planning and Design of the Muswell Hill Odeon Complex 1935-36 by Susan Heathcote (Open University 1980)

An Edwardian Architect in London – John Samuel Alder 1847-1919 by Anthony Hunt (Architectural Association; five volumes 1993)

Cranbourne Road N 10: Original House Names and Numbers; also Curzon and Cecil by Joy Nichol (1999) (HHS Archives)

Secondary

Church and institutional histories

The Church on the Hill – a short history of St James by G Watson & L Kent (1951)

The Story of St James's School by I T Plant (1950)

Muswell Hill Methodist Church 1899-1949 (1949)

The History of St Andrew's Church 1899-1950 by H E Boisseau (1950)

Muswell Hill Baptist Church 1902-1977 by Donald Hardie (1977)

Our Lady of Muswell – A History 1939-1988 by Oonagh Gay (1998)

Muswell Hill Cottage Home for Girls Report 1905 (HHS Archive)

Muswell Hill Electric Theatre and Summerland Gardens: programme 1913

Muswell Hill Golf Club Centenary History 1893-1993 by John S Henderson (1993)

St James Parish Magazine July 1892 (LMA)

Hornsey Historical Society Bulletin articles

Joan Schwitzer:	Before urbanisation: the thoughts of Chairman Cachemaille	(No.12 1976)
Joan Schwitzer:	The Lost Houses of Hornsey No.6: Colethall House, Fortis Green	(No.13 1977)
Reginald Smith:	A tour round Muswell Hill and Fortis Green	(No.14 1977)
Joan Schwitzer:	W B Tegetmeier 1816-1912	(No.17 1978)
John Barrie & Dot Woodrow: A half century of transport in Hornsey		(No.19 1979)
Joan Schwitzer:	A History of Bond & White 1879-1979	(No.20 1979)

Rhona Goss-Custard:	Kings House School	(No.21 1980)
Malcolm Stokes:	Highgate Hunting Ground	(No.25 1984)
Jan Marsh:	An Old Boundary?	(No.25 1984)
Richard Samways:	Local Democrats – The Hornsey Vestry in Action c. 1740-1800	(No.28 1987)
Anne Trevett:	Rookfield Garden Estate	(No.29 1988)
Bernard Brown:	'Damn Yankees' and 'the Met' 1829-1986	(No.29 1988)
John Adlington:	Harold Guylee Chester, philanthropist 1887-1973	(No.30 1989)
Clyde Binfield:	All Muswell Hill and Little Betty Martin: the establishing of a Congregational Church 1890-1929	(No.31 1990)
Jill Hetherington:	'The Muswell Hill Outrage' – a London suburban crime of the 1880s	(No.31 1990)
Joan Schwitzer:	The Journal of Thomas Moore 1779-1856	(No.32 1991)
Ken Gay:	Rabbits and Pheasants in Muswell Hill – Mr Cable's reminiscences (1926)	(No.32 1991)
Ben Travers (ed):	No.33 (1992) entitled *Home Fires – A North London Suburb at War*	
Ruth Phillips:	Charles Darwin and the Tegetmeiers	(No.34 1993)
Jules Kosky:	The Sage of Muswell Hill: William Ernest Henley (1849-1903)	(No.36 1995)
Joyce Horner:	Grove Lodge, Muswell Hill	(No.37 1996)
Ken Gay:	Local Surgeries	(No.38 1997)
Ken Gay:	Robert Paul, Film Pioneer of Muswell Hill	(No.38 1997)
Mrs Howe:	Charles Rook, builder of Muswell Hill	(No.39 1998)
Ken Gay:	The (mostly lost) Cinemas of Haringey	(No.40 1999)

Books relating to Muswell Hill and Hornsey

William Robinson:	*A History of Tottenham* (2nd ed. 1840)
Cornelius Nicholson:	*Scraps of History of a Northern Suburb of London* (1879)
William J Pinks:	*The History of Clerkenwell* (2nd ed. 1880)
John Lloyd:	*The History, Topography and Antiquities of Highgate (1888)*
R O Sherington:	*The Story of Hornsey* (1904)

R Mudie-Smith:	*The Religious Life of London* (1904)
Frederic Harrison:	*Autobiographical Memoirs:* Volume One (1911)
J F Connolly & J Harvey Bloom:	*An Island of Clerkenwell* (1933)
F M W Draper:	*Muswell Farm; or Clerkenwell Detached* (1934) (off-print from Trans. LMAS New series Vol VI – Part IV)
F M W Draper:	*Muswell Hill Past and Present* (1935)
S J Madge:	*The Origin of the Name of Hornsey* (1936)
S J Madge:	*The Early Records of Harringay alias Hornsey* (1938)
S J Madge:	*The Mediaeval Records of Harringay alias Hornsey* (1939)
English Place Name Society:	*Place Names in Middlesex* (1942)
F M W Draper:	*Literary Associations of Muswell Hill* (1948)
F M W Draper:	*Muswell Rhymes* (1948)
John Connell:	*W E Henley* (1949)
Michael Robbins:	*Middlesex* (1953)

Victoria County History of Middlesex Vol. I (1969), Vol. V (1976), Vol. VI (1980)

Caroline Neuberg:	*The Cranley Gardens Hoard* (1972) (off-print of Transactions of LMAS Volume 23 Part 2)
Ron Carrington:	*Alexandra Park & Palace* (1975)
Charles Landstone:	*I Gate-Crashed* (1976)
John Richardson:	*Highgate: Its History from the 15th Century* (1983)
Dolly Shepherd:	*When the Chute Went Up* (1984; 2nd ed. 1996)
David E Freeman:	*Looking at Muswell Hill* (1984)
Joan Schwitzer (ed.):	*Lost Houses of Haringey* (1986)
Ken Gay:	*A Walk Around Muswell Hill* (1987)
Ken Gay:	*From Forest to Suburb: the story of Hornsey retold* (1988)
Ken Gay & Dick Whetstone:	*From Highgate to Hornsey: a portrait in old picture postcards* (1989)
Robert Williams:	*Herbert Collins 1885-1975: architect and worker for peace* (1985)
Ben Travers:	*The Book of Crouch End* (1990)

Ken Gay:	*Palace on the Hill: a history of Alexandra Palace and Park* (1992)
Ian Murray:	*Haringey Before Our Time: a brief history* (1993)
Reg Davies:	*Rails to the People's Palace* (3rd ed. 1994)
Joan Schwitzer & Ken Gay:	*Highgate & Muswell Hill*; Chalford Archive Photographs series (1995)
Jack Whitehead:	*The Growth of Muswell Hill* (1995)
Joan Schwitzer (ed.):	*People and Places: lost estates in Highgate, Hornsey and Wood Green* (1996)
Ken Gay:	*Hornsey & Crouch End*: Chalford Archive Photographs Series (1998)

Books relating to London

Donald Olsen:	*The Growth of Victorian London* (1976)
John Richardson:	*London and Its People* (1995)
Bridget Cherry & Nikolaus Pevsner:	*Buildings of England: London 4: North* (1998)
Stephen Inwood:	*A History of London* (1998)
Francis Sheppard:	*London: A History* (1998)
Alex Werner (ed.):	*London Bodies* (1998)
Andrew Saint (ed.):	*London Suburbs* (1999)

Other Books

Charles E Lee:	*The Early Motor Bus* (1964)
Richard Morris:	*Churches in the Landscape* (1987)
F M L Thompson:	*The Rise of Respectable Society 1830-1900* (1988)
Rodney Dale:	*Early Cars* (1994)
N Johanessen:	*Telephone Boxes* (1994)

Index